D1626411

95800000192132

TEACHINGS from our ANIMAL SPIRIT GUIDES

TEACHINGS from our ANIMAL SPIRIT GUIDES

HARNESS the POWER of ANIMALS to LIBERATE your SPIRIT

Susie Green

Illustrated by
Csaba Pásztor

CICO BOOKS
LONDON NEW YORK

This edition published in 2021 by CICO Books
An imprint of Ryland Peters & Small Ltd
20–21 Jockey's Fields   341 E 116th St
London WC1R 4BW   New York, NY 10029

First published in 2005 as *Animal Wisdom*

www.rylandpeters.com

10 9 8 7 6 5 4 3 2 1

A CIP catalog record for this book is available from the Library of
Congress and the British Library.

ISBN: 978 1 80065 013 8

Printed in China

Editor: Liz Dean
Designer: David Fordham
Illustrator: Csaba Pásztor

Art director: Sally Powell
Head of production: Patricia Harrington
Publishing manager: Penny Craig
Publisher: Cindy Richards

CONTENTS

Susie Green is the author of the bestselling *Animal Messages* and *Bird Messages*, both published by CICO Books, and the critically acclaimed work *Dogs in Art*, published by Reaktion. Susie has written extensively about pets and their wilder cousins for British national newspapers the *Guardian* and the *Daily Mail*, and specialist animal magazines. She lives in Kent, UK.

Csaba Pásztor studied natural history illustration at the Royal College of Art, London. He is a master of many disciplines: illustration for books, carvings in stone and wood, furniture-making, and interior design, including *tromp l'oeil* paintings. He also taught life drawing and anatomy. Csaba loves and respects animals, as the beautiful lino cuts reproduced in this book demonstrate.

INTRODUCTION:
ANIMAL AFFINITY

Humankind is so new to earth. Our first footprints fell here only one hundred and thirty thousand years ago, but animals have been here since the dawn of time. Spider has spun her silken weave for four hundred million years. Tortoise has plodded over hot sand for two hundred and twenty million. Pig first rooted in moist, rich soil thirty-seven million years ago, while even Tiger, a relative newcomer to the world, has patroled the eastern jungles for one-and-a-half million years.

What incredible powers, sagacity, and immense knowledge all these creatures possess. What immense knowledge they must have accrued. Animals have always devised ways to exist, even within the most harsh or unforgiving of environments. Some animals, like Squid, live on the ocean's floor where the water's pressure would crush us. Cold-blooded Frog produces an anti-freeze glycerol so that she may pass winters of twenty-two degrees Fahrenheit (-6° C) in comfortable torpor. Cheetah sprints at seventy miles per hour (110 km/h), the speed limit on British freeways. Bush Baby can detect the first light of dawn well before the most sophisticated light meter. Dog can smell the bio-chemical changes of cancer – no test devised by man is yet capable of this. And how varied is their social structure: Hyena society is a matriarchy, Meerkat's is a model for the communist ideal, while self-sufficient Panda lives alone in her dense bamboo.

The advent of industrialization and technology has separated us from the natural world and its wisdom. While opening up a degree of choice that is simply staggering, this also traps us in a stress-laden, polluted urban environment. We wonder why we feel tired, sad, or confused. Have we made the right decision out of so many? To have six children or none? Get married, or play the field? How to handle our boss, our landlord, our lover, our ever-burgeoning loan?

We live in a complex and hard world, subject to pressures and dilemmas inconceivable to our ancestors. But their problems were not less than ours, simply different. Prey to vast predators and virulent disease, utterly dependent upon the success of the hunt for continued survival and harassed by inter-tribal warfare, they, too, looked for answers in a harsh world. Most often, they found them in the wisdom of animals. Wolf, for example, was a skilled predator long before humans developed their first primitive hunting skills. In Wyoming, where prairie grass was dominant, Wolf would lower and wave her tail to attract shy but curious Antelope close enough to ambush; Shoshoni Indians observed her success and also lay flat in the grass, waving a strip of hide in imitation and homage to her prowess.

We too can tap into animal wisdom. For every dilemma we face, every problem we must overcome, there is a creature who holds the solution. This book contains the wisdom of a hundred different creatures, although all of course possess much, much more. As you dip into it you may feel drawn to Bear, to Kangaroo, to Crab, and see within their way of living the key to your future path, the answer to your predicament. You can then draw more deeply on their powers and come to know their wisdom better, by dancing them, shapeshifting, and studying their lives in nature (see page 22).

Early man's animistic and Shamanic traditions presume that everything natural upon earth was imbued with spirit – be it the wind whistling through the redwoods, or exotically plumed Parrot – and that these spirits live in another reality, known as the Upper and Lower Worlds. Animal spirits often try to reach out to us when they feel that their own particular magic can help us. We may be familiar with Crow's great black wings beating in the air above us, but when their tip unusually brushes our shoulder, she surely has a message for us. When our dreams are populated by Owl, by Orangutan, or Snake, they, too, wish to speak with us. When we watch a wildlife program and are inexplicably touched or drawn to one particular creature, they are trying to attract our attention and share with us their wisdom.

With this book you can begin to speak their language, translate their messages, and use their wisdom to enhance your life and find a new way forward.

PART ONE

YOUR ANIMALS AS GUIDES

THE LOST COSMOLOGY OF ANIMAL WISDOM

It is a long way from downtown Los Angeles or perfume-laden Provence, from being a Bollywood Hindu or New York WASP, to prehistoric hunter-gatherer man. Yet no matter where we are today, all our ancestors sat around hot-embered fires while hungry beasts prowled in the near darkness, gazing at magical star-studded skies in awe and perplexity and making salutations to shadowy spirits hoping that above all things the hunt – the one thing that stood between them and ultimately, death – would be successful. Prehistoric man understood in an absolutely direct way that alone he could not survive. He knew in every fiber of his body that he was an insignificant fragment of an interdependent whole, and that without the compassion of the essences of earth, sky, and water, the spirits of animals, ancestors and gods, his life force would be extinguished.

In a world where lumps of meat packaged in cellophane lay on bright supermarket shelves for the taking, it is hard to identify with the raw emotion that coursed constantly through our ancestors' veins: surges of adrenaline and ever-increasing panic if the hunt failed; gnawing, indescribable hunger like a ravening beast waiting for his chance to devour them; terror when voracious epidemics burgeoned. But also, a sublime wonder at the mystery of life and the ways of the spirits and essences who held equally the outcome of the hunt and the prognosis of a smallpox patient in their hands. Ancient man had no technology with which to moderate his environment, to turn the balance of the hunt in his favor. But he did possess literally the most power-full tool of all, and one that is still at our disposal, if we choose to use it: the ability to alter his consciousness and enter the lost cosmology of non-ordinary reality. And, once there, influence the train of events in earth's ordinary reality.

THE SHAMANIC WORLD VIEW

Whether its peoples lived in the frozen wastes of the Siberian tundra, the sultry jungles of the southern Americas, or the temperate forests of Europe, the archaic mythology, religions, and traditions of almost every culture refer back to a paradisal age now lost to humankind.

Although the details differ, in essence the cosmology is always the same: a Lower World, Middle World (earth), and an Upper World exist, connected by a central axis or meeting point. In this non-ordinary reality, the first magical creation of earthly space, dwelt the essences and spirits of all nature. Humankind dwelt in mystical solidarity and harmony with all the creatures of sky, forest, ocean, and soil. They were as one, at peace. Human creatures understood quite naturally the language of the winged, furred, and other beings with whom they dwelt, partook of their wisdom and knowledge, and were intimate with the secrets of all nature. They were able to slip easily from one plane to another and communicate freely with the gods and spirits above, and the souls of their ancestors and others below.

But man always falls from this wondrous situation of grace and becomes "what he is today – mortal, sexed, obliged to work to feed himself, and at enmity with the animals."[1] In Biblical traditions this awe-full catastrophe is enacted by Eve's expulsion from the Garden of Eden after so humanly giving in to temptation by biting into the apple of knowledge.

Although we can no longer perceive these other worlds, they still exist. The spirit of Thunder, Dragonfly, Beaver, and even the Sun still have their own consciousness, wants, desires, and needs. And, like the gods of the ancient Greek and Roman pantheons, they can sustain human life or, in a moment of jealousy and capriciousness, destroy it.

Humanity, and the individuals who comprise it are merely a tiny, infinitesimal part of a whole in which everything is interdependent, the earth part of a larger whole which includes the Upper and Lower Worlds which "represent the true nature of things and the true causes of events in this world."[2]

The rivers of this world cannot be poisoned with pollutants without the fish who inhabit those waters taking the toxins into their own bodies. We feed on the fish and the toxins lodge in our cells, damaging us in innumerable ways If the Goddess of the Animals is angry with humankind, she keeps Deer in her world and the hunt will fail and the tribe starve. For everything that changes must in turn change something else.

WHAT IS A SHAMAN?

Shamans are interpreters of dreams, social workers, mystics, diviners, herbalists, advisors, and protectors who posses the power to combat evil spirits and save their tribe from famine, starvation, disease, distress, and war. Shamans devote their lives to spiritual practice and almost daily undergo psychic and physical rigors that others would find simply unendurable.

They practice in places as diverse as the imperial courts of ancient China and the tribal hunter-gatherer societies of the Amazonian basin to down-town New York, but none attain spiritual authority until they have undergone a rigorous initiation in non-ordinary worlds and are able to journey to them at will. These worlds are not a figment of the Shaman's imagination or a hallucination, but simply another world in which the spirit inhabitants are as alive as the humans and other creatures in ordinary reality. In our everyday lives, we cannot see the ultraviolet patterns gloriously painted on the petals of many flowers, but Butterfly can. We cannot sense the kinetic electric fields formed when water moves through the earth's magnetic field, although Ray can. We cannot see non-ordinary reality – but the Shaman can.

To access the realm of animal spirits the Shaman enters an altered, ecstatic state of consciousness (usually referred to as a Shamanic State of Consciousness – SSC – to differentiate it from other altered states such as those experienced during meditation) which changes his perceptive range, or cognition.

While science has caught up with Ray and Butterfly and proved to its satisfaction that ultraviolet and kinetic electric fields exist, it has yet, however, to catch up with the Shaman.

Unlike an individual who enters a meditative state, the Shaman at will enters a SSC, specifically to visit the usually hidden Upper and Lower Worlds. He is in control of his experience there in the same way as we may control our responses in ordinary reality. If we walk to the store we do not know if we will bump into a friend, trip on a paving stone, or buy a new coat on impulse, but how we deal with the people and incidents that occur as we "journey" is up to us. And so it is with the Shaman.

THE FIRST SHAMANS

In Shamanic mythology, the first Shamans came to help humankind in need. Usually men, although sometimes women, these humans received their divine Shamanic right directly from their supreme celestial god or his emissary Eagle, bird of the sun, embodiment of solar energy, and were made so supremely puissant that they "really flew through the clouds on their horses and performed miracles their present-day descendants are incapable of repeating."[3] Arrogant and proud, they declared their powers boundless, and challenged the very gods who fashioned them. Khara-Gyrgän, First Shaman of the Siberian Buryat, asserted he could set free the soul of a young girl imprisoned by the Buryat's supreme being. The Shaman flew to the Upper World on his drum and discovered his god holding the soul in a bottle, its escape through the neck blocked by a divine finger. Khara-Gyrgän changed his form to that of a spider and stung his god, who in surprised pain at once pulled his finger from the bottle, setting the soul free.

Angered at Khara-Gyrgän's temerity the god vastly reduced his powers to those still marvelous abilities that Shamans attain and exercise today.

A Tibetan Shaman with a traditional drum and thigh bone, Manang, Nepal.

THE SHAMAN'S TASKS

The Shaman is his tribe's representative in non-ordinary reality. In the hunting cultures in which Shamanism was virtually universally adopted, and more particularly in the northern hemisphere, his most vital mission is negotiating with the Great Goddess of all the Animals – or, more rarely, a Beast Master – who holds within her the spirit and essence of all the earth's creatures. These spirits will release a certain number of animals to the hunters in ordinary reality, but only sufficient to sustain life and no more. In return they demand reverence for themselves and the spirits of the animals, respect for cosmic and social harmony, and social morality toward the flesh-and-blood animals of earth.

When starvation threatens communities in Siberia, the Shaman must journey before his villagers to the very bottom of the ocean. There, he must entreat Takánakapsâluk, Mother of the Sea Beasts, to have compassion and save their lives by releasing Seal. A truly powerful Shaman dives down a tunnel beneath his igloo and reaches Takánakapsâluk's home in the Lower World immediately – other Shamans, who may be less talented, must descend through the earth and the depths of the dark ocean, facing terrible obstacles which he must then overcome.

As she is ireful, a great wall rises before her house and the Shaman must knock it down in order to gain entry. Takánakapsâluk is dirty, slovenly; her hair hangs limply over her face – a sign that humankind's sins and their breaking of taboos are taking their toll. In revenge she keeps her marine creatures in a pool next to her and the Shaman, while combing her hair, must call upon all his powers to appease her anger.

At last, she opens the pool and lets the animals free. The villagers hear their movements at the bottom of the sea, and soon afterwards the Shaman's gasping breathing, as if he were emerging from the surface of the water. A long silence follows. Finally, the Shaman speaks and demands that the villagers confess their sins, which they freely do, and repent. Then Seal may come, and the villagers may eat.

SHAMANISM AND HEALING

Another vital Shamanic function is healing. Many Shamanistic traditions believe that from childhood every human being has a guardian animal, often called a power animal, a name which core shamanism in the West tends to use for all our helping animal spirits. This adjective does not mean that the animal is powerful in the sense that it is large and strong, but that its own specific powers, be they those of Weasel or Wolf, are available to a person. The presence of this guardian keeps the person it protects healthy because it "provides a power-full body that resists the intrusion of external forces"[4] such as disease, prevents depression and material or emotional misfortune, and bestows well-being which encompasses happy friendships, eating well, and success in work. For various reasons, however, the power animal may abandon her human (see pages 22, 31) leading to tribulations of various kinds, and the Shaman must travel to non-ordinary reality to reclaim the power animal and so heal the person.

The Shaman may also need to practice soul retrieval. A person may have many souls, and the root cause of serious illness is often attributed to the loss of the soul, which normally descends to the Lower World only on death. It may have been corrupted, alienated, or captured, and the Shaman who through the experience of his own initiation (see page 16) may retrieve it through battle, negotiation, or simply by discovering its whereabouts. Without his soul the patient may die, so the Shaman's task is an arduous one.

BECOMING A SHAMAN

Since the time of the First Shamans (see page 13) Shamans have been recruited in different ways. Some inherit the calling from their family, whose ancestors had been chosen by the spirits. Some are singled out by spirits who make their wishes clear using various signs, such as striking them with lightning, a signal indication of the celestial origin of Shamanic powers. Many fall seriously ill with baneful diseases such as smallpox and, while unconscious, come to understand what the spirits require of them – others may receive their calling in their dreams. Candidates who resist the spirits' call – for the way of the Shaman is a truly hard one and not all wish to take it – can suddenly appear to go mad, running naked to the mountains and living on soil for days, spending weeks on a tree branch, and returning to their village unkempt and babbling wildly. The spirits may harass their chosen one, sometimes even threatening him with death until he agrees to initiation, after which he is restored to perfect health. Finally, there are those who voluntarily take up this vocation, but they are destined never to attain the supreme powers of the chosen.

Yet no matter how Shamans are recruited, none gain their spiritual authority or may practice until they have successfully undergone what is often a grueling initiation while unconscious. In the majority of cultures the future Shaman experiences having his flesh peeled from his body until only his sundered bones remain – the fundamental symbols of existence and life for societies dependent upon hunting. The candidate is then reassembled and remade, stronger and more powerful than before. These experiences are internalized, for he simultaneously suffers a dismantling of his psyche and undergoes tremendous human suffering so that when he regains consciousness his nature is truly new: he is reborn as a Shaman. During this process he also meets assistants and tutelary spirits and his animal guardians, without whose wisdom and guidance he would be lost in an alien geography of place and mind.

THE INITIATION OF DIVER

The initiation of an Avam Samoyed Shaman, known as Huottarie or Diver after his rebirth, is one of the very few recorded in detail by early anthropologists. These extracts contain crucial elements of Diver's initiation and show graphically the seamless correspondence between earthly reality and the Lower and Upper Worlds which makes journeying so fruitful.

Diver was unconscious, suffering from smallpox when the spirit of the disease revealed to him that he was to become a Shaman and his initiation took place. Almost immediately, the Lord of the Underworld gave him two animal spirit helpers, Ermine and Mouse. Healing being intrinsic to a Shaman, Ermine and Mouse first took Diver to a tented encampment where he met the Lord of Madness and the Lords of Nervous Diseases, and learned to diagnose and cure all mankind's ailments.

Shamans must also be able to sing and chant lustily to call upon the spirits, so next Mouse and Ermine guided him to the Land of Shamanesses who strengthened his throat and voice.

On an island in the middle of the Nine Seas, Diver was given a birch by The Lord of the Tree to make the bodies of three ceremonial drums: one for helping women in childbirth, another for curing the sick, and the third for finding those who were lost in the snow. He was then inculcated with the medicinal properties of the earth's plants.

Non-ordinary reality contains within itself the secrets of future on earth, which is why our animal guides can give us messages when we journey, as can animals in ordinary reality, because they are the earthly representatives of divine spirits. Diver's message was that he would marry three women on earth. In keeping with the powers given to him during his initiation, Diver cured three orphans by driving the spirit of smallpox from them and, as prophesied, married all three.

Various bird spirits now also came to help Diver, and flew him to the Place of Seven Stones, where he learned their mineral secrets.

Finally, and most importantly, Ermine and Mouse took him to a bright cave covered with mirrors. Here he met two personifications of the Mother of the Animals, who although human in form were covered in reindeer fur. Both gave birth to reindeer so that the reindeer might be released for the earthly hunt, and the animal mothers gave Diver one reindeer hair each, which he could call upon when he needed help in procuring the hunt. This cave exists in ordinary reality, and when Diver must Shamanize for the hunt he always turns toward it.

Having been given wonderful wisdoms and extraordinary skills it was time for Diver to be remade, to be forged both physically and psychically. Deep in the bowels of a mountain the architect of this transformation, a blacksmith, worked naked. Diver experienced the terror of dying as the blacksmith severed his head, chopped up his body, and boiled these pieces in a giant cauldron for three years. The blacksmith then retrieved Diver's bones from a river and coated them with flesh before forging his head on an anvil and changing his eyes, so that when he journeyed or Shamanized he could see with mystical eyes, rather than those of earth, and pierced his ears so that he would understand the language of plants.

A new man, tempered and strong like steel, full of wisdoms from the dawn of time, in non-ordinary reality Diver found himself on the top of a mountain, while simultaneously on earth he awoke healed, and from then on was able to sing, dance and Shamanize indefinitely without tiring.

FROM SHAMANISM, MIRCEA ELIADE, QUOTING A A POPOV

BATEK INITIATION
SHAMANISM HAS EVOLVED IN INTIMATE RAPPORT WITH
ECOLOGY OF PLACE, AS THIS QUITE DIFFERENT SHAMANIC
INITIATION SHOWS.

The Bateks, who must share their land in Malaysia with predatory Tiger, concentrate on investing their Shamans with her power by another universal Shamanic practice – taking another creature's form to partake of its wisdom and energy. In Batek cosmology, the Lower World is a maze of limestone caves inhabited by *hala'*, or supernatural, tigers who posses the immortal shadow souls of dead Batek Shamans. *Hala'* tigers are the guardians, helpers, and teachers of their human descendants. Again showing correspondence between ordinary and non-ordinary reality these caves, known as Batu Balok, are situated on the banks of the Palah river and certainly as late as the 1960s flesh-and-blood tigers made them their own. From the center of these caves rises a pillar, the central core around which lie the Lower, Middle, and Upper Worlds of Shamanic cosmology.

When the Batek die, the soul rises on clouds of perfumed incense to the Upper World where it is transformed into a *hala'*, a superhuman or spirit with two bodies, one a young and vigorous version of their earthly self, and the other a glorious, powerful tiger.

To become a Shaman and help his tribe, a Batek must brave the dark of the graveyard seven days after his relative's death and await his appearance in tiger form. When this fearsome spirit arrives, he must blow magical incense over him to cause him to take on human form so that he may teach the would-be Shaman his songs, spells, and the secrets of sending his shadow-soul silently through the world so that he may hear secrets being told at other campfires and how to journey to non-ordinary realities. Finally he gives the novice a tiger body of his own and shows him how to step into and use the mighty feline's extraordinary powers. The Batek is now a Shaman holding the powers of the world's supreme hunter, a supernatural warrior equipped to destroy anything which might harm his tribe and who works to keep their spiritual identity whole.

TAPPING INTO SHAMANIC WISDOM IN AN INDUSTRIALIZED SOCIETY

Hunting dominates Shamanic practice in societies where it is key for survival. In societies where warfare is an integral component of life, then that too becomes central. As societies move from hunting and intertribal strife to farming and herding, domestic animals began to be included in the tribe's rites and, as nations began to arise, a whole range of other elements crept in.

Shamanism, wherever it occurs and whatever its central preoccupation, possesses key elements. Shamans all travel to non-ordinary reality in ecstatic trance, are guided and assisted by animal spirits, and gain wisdom from various other divinities and spirits of the natural world. It is a plastic practice, melding to the cultural milieu in which it operates where it is interpreted and evaluated in different ways. For people living in contemporary industrialized societies, the rituals specific to any tribal culture, historic or current, can have no inner meaning. They have no relevance to the way we live, the situation we find ourselves in and so can never be ours. To perform them would be meaningless.

However, like millions of people before us we can take Shamanic practice and make it ours, shaping its rituals to reflect the concerns of our own lives and of a world very much changed from that which was familiar to our ancestors of even one hundred years ago.

We do not need to be initiated as Shamans to practice Shamanism. Although the way of the Shaman is arduous and rigorous – he must devote himself to psychically grueling spiritual practice, and it is not for the majority of humankind whether they dwell in the Amazonian jungle or New York City – it is simply a matter of degree. Buddhist monks also devote their lives to spiritual practice, by meditating for long periods, studying the *sutras*, and engaging in spiritual debate. This life, too, is not for everyone, but millions of people worldwide practice Buddhism and

Shamans of Tungusta, Russia, illustrated in 1894.

derive intense spiritual solace and meaning from it. And so it is with Shamanism.

The ability to experience ecstatic trance is fundamental to the human condition. The Shaman may journey more frequently than the rest of his tribe and perform arduous work on their behalf when he does so, but very often they, too, can travel to non-ordinary reality, receive messages in dreams or through earthly signs, and be blessed with animal guardians who guide them and mind their welfare. Like Shamans, through visualization, we too can fly like the wind through a blue-purple sky, descend to the Lower World, speak freely with the spirits of wind and fire, the sprites of stream and wood, and regain that paradisal time when we could speak with animals. We can all discover our power animals who walk by our side and imbue us with overwhelming well-being. We can learn to interpret their messages in dreams and in terrestrial reality, as well as those from other animal spirits who come at a particular time for a particular reason. And we can tap into the wisdom of animal spirits when we need to.

All it takes to practice Shamanism is time, the honoring of nature on earth and its spirits in non-ordinary reality, and a measure of love and determination.

HONORING NATURE AND ANIMALS

At the heart of the Shamanic world view is honoring and respecting every aspect of nature. In particular, it sees no divide between the soul and essence of man and that of beast. Their relationship is that of kin. Many societies, including the majority of Native North American Indians, had no word to classify animals *per se*; they were simply other people. Because of this it was unthinkable to waste nature's bounty, to hunt for any other reason than need. If an animal died that the tribe might live, be clothed, and have bone for arrow heads, its sacrifice was revered.

Most other cultures have not esteemed the natural world. It has been looked upon simply as something to plunder and wantonly destroy. Yet animals and the natural environment are as intrinsic to our very survival as they ever were. Because much of humankind is now separated from nature in huge urban conglomerations, it squanders what remains of its largesse without understanding where it has come from or the consequences of so doing.

Domestic farm animals, tractable cousins of their proud wild forebears of jungle and forest, still feed and clothe us, and provide us with everything from lanolin to soothe our skin to the bristles to brush our hair, but far from being revered for the wonders they give us, the lot of these creatures is to be treated with contempt.

Large, meat-rich sharks whose skin could be used as leather are wantonly taken from the deep, their fins – the least nutritious part of their entire bodies – cut off to make sharks' fin soup and their still-living selves thrown back into the sea to die in pain and indescribable misery, regarded as living garbage. Not surprisingly, many shark species are now endangered and the seas become emptier every day. When an entire species dies, which now happens many times a day, every day, we are the losers. Their wisdom is gone forever. It can never be reclaimed, and we are the weaker for it.

Many cowards hunt "for pleasure", killing Wolf from helicopters using infrared and telescopic sights on a gun, degrading humanity and degenerating the environment by disturbing the balance of nature. Since wolf packs have been re-established in Yellowstone Park, all its flora and fauna are flourishing in ways that were unimaginable even twenty years ago and that, surely, is as it should be.

Practicing Shamanism, becoming intimately involved with the spirits of nature, our animal guides, and seeing their reflection in the terrestrial world around us, causes profound psychic shifts. Being part of nature is no longer a theoretical position but an inner actuality. Deep within we know that damaging and disrespecting nature not only harms the environment, but ourselves. Gradually it becomes automatic for us to honor all living creatures, to consider the results of our actions, and respect the oneness of what is now a very ill Gaia.

In the twenty-first century this means preserving the lands and space that are wild creatures' birthright, and fighting for the retention of untamed wilderness everywhere in the world. It means refusing to eat factory-farmed animals, or eating foods such as shark's fin soup. It means never buying products tested on animals, and abjuring waste. We can make a difference and heal not only ourselves but the world.

ANIMAL GUIDES, HELPERS, AND MESSENGERS

Cities divorce us from nature. Airplanes, road traffic, and sirens drown out the songs of the few birds who eke out an existence on window boxes and in small suburban gardens. Our feet, insulated by layers of concrete and asphalt, never touch earth, leaving us ungrounded. Dogs – our oldest and most faithful animal guides, both in myth and reality – are more often excluded from city centers, bars, and even parks. Even if our conscious minds do not admit it, our souls bleed at this loss. It is perhaps not surprising, then, that the idea of having animal guides resonates strongly with people who live in Western society. Connecting with them and learning to recognize the messages that earthly animals are sending us, particularly those who still live amongst us such as Raccoon, Crow, Fox, and Mouse, help redress that balance and make us whole.

Core Shamanic practice in the West and particularly in North America makes particular reference to finding our animal guides and keeping them with us. Many cultures, such as those of the Jívaro in South America, believe that at least one power animal is with us from birth whether we know it or not, for without their protection we would not reach the age of six or seven. As we grow older, desertion by our animal guides, which happens for various reasons, can leave us feeling sad, depressed, de-energized, or ill. As their beneficence also bestows overall well-being, their absence can also be responsible for misfortune. For animal guides do not necessarily stay with us for life. They may come to us for a few years, even a few weeks depending on how we treat them, for remember that they too have their own desires and agendas (see also Deepening Your Relationship With Your Animal Guide, page 31).

Animal guides reveal themselves to Shamans during their initiation, as Ermine and Mouse did to Diver (see page 16) but there are many other ways to become aware of them, as we will see below.

Whichever way you take, there is one overriding fact to take into account: your guide chooses to come to you or is given to you by some other superior divinity such as the Lord of the Lower World. You cannot choose your animal guide. Some individuals are disappointed to discover that their guardian is Ant or Sloth instead of a creature they consider more glamorous such as Wolf or Wild Horse, and, rejecting their guardian, endeavor to contact another which they consider more charismatic. This attempt will surely fail.

We may be able to call on a specific animal spirit when we have a heartfelt need for its wisdom if our plea is eloquent, but this is not the case with a guardian. If you reject this helping spirit you may lose her forever, and perhaps not be chosen by, or given, another.

Every creature has its own special wisdom and magic and none is better than another – they are simply different. Each one is absolutely essential to the web of life on earth and the greater cosmology of non-ordinary reality. Ant, for example, is tiny but mighty. One lone individual can carry a leaf thousands of times her size over rocky terrain, or stalk and kill with a power as awesome as Tiger. Ant farmers grow fungus to sustain the collective, while architects create complex galleried homes with vaulted ceilings. Ant, like every living being is simply *extra*-ordinary. If she chooses you, you are privileged indeed.

HOW TO DISCOVER YOUR ANIMAL GUIDE

HOW TO JOURNEY

Journeying is to send your spirit, your very essence, deliberately and purposefully into non-ordinary reality, into the world we can only see when we let our minds free. This world is at the heart of Shamanic practice.

For many people the first journey they take will be to discover their animal guide. But before you journey, you must learn how to enter the Upper and Lower Worlds. Western core Shamanism has evolved a way that is accessible to us all. Below is an overview of these techniques.

When passing into the paradisal worlds of non-ordinary reality, Shamans use an opening that exists here on earth, and so may we. The portals for Lower World journeys might be a cave filled with glorious stalactites and stalagmites behind the rushing coolness of a waterfall, the descending roots of a mighty tree, the crack between two rocks, a deep well, a rabbit hole, or a sea grotto. The only thing that is important is that you feel a real affinity to it. It could be a mighty oak you have always loved, somewhere you fell in love with in a faraway clime, or a place you pass every day. Whether you could enter it in earthly reality is not important, for your spirit can go wherever you direct it. (See the exercises on pages 24–27.)

An engraving depicting Yakhout Shamans in Mongolia.

DRUMMING

In many cultures altered perception is brought about by the sonic driving force of repetitive drumming, rattling and, sometimes, chanting. Tribal Shamans have often been given the wood for the body of their drums during their initiation. Very often it may come from the embodiment on earth of the World Tree, which connects the three worlds of Shamanistic cosmology. This means that its simple presence transports them to the place where all worlds collide, allowing them to slip from one to another.

The sound of the drum is musical magic and we, too, can employ it. A single beat contains many different frequencies and so transmits impulses through many neural pathways in the brain. Repetitive rhythmic drumming stimulates the brain, which may account for their ability to induce a Shamanic state of consciousness. Two hundred and five to two hundred and twenty beats per minute seems to effect this most readily. When you first want to journey, however, you may not know anyone with a drum let alone a consummate drummer. A wonderful alternative is a drumming CD. Although a CD can never impart the immediacy and excitement of live drumming, it can still transport you, and features a "call-back" rhythm at the end as a reminder to return to earthly reality.

EXERCISE 1

This exercise helps you become familiar with entering the Lower and Upper Worlds, after which you can practice the second exercise, opening up to animal communication.

ENTERING THE LOWER WORLD

1 Close your eyes and imagine passing through your entrance and, as you do so, create a tunnel in your mind. This is your passageway to the mystical Lower World. Remember that you are not going into earthly soil and rock, but somewhere quite different. For some, this

process is almost automatic, as if using a skill that had been theirs forever but remained dormant. Others find that their passageway does not at first come unbidden, and they must make a strong effort to fashion it in their mind. This does not have any significance or make the experience any less valuable. You have made a conscious decision to visit the Lower World and if envisaging your passageway takes effort, this simply emphasizes your control over your journey.

2 Where does the tunnel go? The tunnel may go on for mile after mile, you may fly through it at the speed of light or walk slowly, absorbing every detail of texture on its walls. It may move in vivid zigzags, be a downward chute, a parting of the waters. It may be dark rock or glittering crystal, it may be luminescent or dim. You may feel it rather than see it, perhaps the passage is dark but air rushes softly by your face. When you feel you are coming to the end of your tunnel, imagine an opening and the sensation or sight of light. This is the Lower World.

3 Familiarize yourself with your portal and tunnel before traveling further. Visit them several times on different occasions until you feel happy and confident. Turn round and return to earth. That when you do emerge from your passageway into the light of the Lower World, which might be brilliant sunlight, soft twilight, or a haze of blue, rose, or gold, you will feel at ease.

ENTERING THE UPPER WORLD
Entering the Upper World involves taking paths to the sky where you may breach its fabric – perhaps through the light of the Pole Star or the edge between sunset and a mountain top. These routes may be the misty smoke which rises from burning, the smell of perfumed incense rising in the air, a shaft of shining sunlight, a silvery moonbeam, a vine stretching to the sky, or an endless ladder. Imagine where these routes contact earth. Perhaps the sunbeam rises from a glade in the woods, the smoke from a bonfire in your garden. Imagine moving with them until you touch the sky and see your opening into another world. As with finding your entrance to the Lower World, practice going to the edge and returning, until you feel confident.

EXERCISE 2
In this exercise, you journey to discover your animal guide. Many people have more than one animal guide. Vasyugan Shaman are often guided in the Lower World by

Bear and fly to the Upper World on Gray Horse; other Shamans report that they have as many as seven guides which may help them in different situations or worlds. If several spirits wait for you, be patient, and let them introduce themselves in their own way. You will soon discover which ones have chosen to guide you.

1 As you do not want the light of ordinary reality to intrude and distract you, you need to make your room soft and dim. It is particularly conducive to journey at night when the earth itself is dark. Start your drumming CD, lie down on the floor in as relaxed a state as possible, your eyes covered with a scarf. If there is danger of disturbing your neighbors, listen to your drumming CD through good-quality headphones. If not, set the volume to a comfortable but not overly loud level and position your head in the optimum spot between the speakers.

2 Imagine going to your now-familiar portal and as you move through your passageway to the Lower World or path to the Upper World (see page 25) send a heartfelt plea that when you reach this new world your animal guide will be there to meet you.

3 This time when you see the light at the end of your tunnel or the break in the fabric of the sky, imagine yourself going through it and becoming part of non-ordinary reality. Don't attempt to move far from your entrance. Look around you quietly and gently, take in your landscape and start to feel the particular quality of this new and amazing land. Usually your guide will look with compassion on your plea and be waiting for you somewhere near your portal. However, as you have never visited this reality before you may not at first recognize her or be certain that she is your guide. Ask again from your heart that she gives you a sign. Tiger might nuzzle your hand, Wolf might lick your face, Bee might dance for you. Any spirit might frisk and induce you to frolic with her. She might appear and disappear several times. Acknowledge her presence and spend the rest of this momentous journey starting to become friends.

4 Perhaps no animal spirit is waiting for you, or those that are give you no special sign. However, as you move a little into your new world you might find that you

are flying on Bat, Horse, or Swan. Your guide is making her presence clear and is cementing your relationship by showing you a little of her world. If you cannot sense your guide, be patient; call out sincerely and she will make herself known. If she does not it may be that you are not receptive or open enough at this time to observe her. She may be there but perhaps you cannot see her, perhaps a part of you doubts her. Spend a little time getting to know your new world and when you journey there next time you will feel more confident, more at ease, and able to accept all its wondrous possibilities.

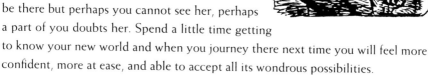

5 When you hear the call-back beat on your CD, ask your guardian to take you back to your portal. You may find you fly together and are there in an instant, or that it suddenly appears before you. You may walk with your guardian by your side, or run through the air. If you have not yet discovered your guardian, all you need do is visualize your portal and begin to walk through it. You will soon be back in earthly reality.

OTHER WAYS OF FINDING YOUR ANIMAL GUIDES AND DRAWING ON ANIMAL POWER

DREAMING
When we dream, we regain paradise and can again talk with the animals. In "dream time", chronological time no longer exists and direct contact with spirits and divinities is again ours – a perfect environment for your animal guide to inhabit.

As we awake, our dreams can slip away unnoticed like phantoms in bright sunshine. However, if when you awake you hold onto the thoughts in your mind and replay your dream, perhaps writing it down in a journal, over a period of just a few weeks you will be able to recall them quite naturally.

Before you slide under cool sheets or nestle under your soft duvet for the night, focus your mind and ask your animal guide to reveal herself. She may not do this the first time you ask, or the second, but if you ask sincerely in time she will, and her image will be lucid and unmistakable.

It is wise to practice dream recall even if you are already

aware of the identity of your animal guide, for other animal spirits also find this a convenient medium for delivering messages. It is not only our longer-term guardians who speak with us – any animal spirit may see that we are in need of help or inspiration and come to show us a way forward that may be particular to their own magical qualities.

DANCING AND SHAPESHIFTING

Dancing is part of a wider phenomenon that we might call shapeshifting. We all shapeshift to a degree, we are one shape or persona when we deal with our bank manager, another on a moonlit walk with a lover. We can project our presence when we walk into a room or become unnoticeable. When we do this we are altering our energies in specific ways, and we are quite capable of altering them in much more extreme ways.

Shamans have always taken on the image of animal spirits in dance, in movement and in costume to conjure their energy, to partake of their power and wisdom, and to become as one with them as a preparation for their ecstatic journey. Like the Batek Shaman who takes the form of Tiger and her powers, so other Shamans take possession of the powers of their assistants.

Their extant costumes show images of their animal assistants. The Mongolian Buryat Shaman, putting himself in contact with a host of animal spirits in his world, wears a two-horned iron cap from which hang "silk, cotton, broadcloth, and velvet ribbons of the color of various game and domestic animals, twisted into the likeness of the snake" ... and "cotton clippings of the color of the squirrel and the yellow weasel."[5] Many Shamans wear the costumes of birds, in particular Eagle and Owl, to take the power of flight, so that they may visit other lands.

Myriad ancient images show human and animal forms merged, of extraordinary masks, of creatures primeval in their power. Many of these, such as the titanic representations of Elk, of Tiger, of anthropomorphic masks hewn on enormous rocks strewn in the waters of the river Amur, are over five thousand years old.

When we dance for an animal, making our body move as its does, pouncing as Wolf might, bending sinuously as Cobra, tiptoeing gently as Deer, we honor that spirit and are usually able to draw some of its wisdom and power into ourselves. When you read the Animal Wisdom profiles in the next part of the book, you might recognize a quality that you feel you lack, and that you wish you could draw upon.

If you feel the need to awaken your sensuality, for example, you might dance like lithe Black Panther, moving stealthily and stretching languorously, and take on more of her persona by wearing black velvet or painting your nails in celebration of her great razor-sharp claws. Whichever Wisdom you wish to draw upon, it is wise to study carefully its spirit's movements and behavior so that when you dance for her you can do so faithfully.

Dancing to discover or reconnect with your animal spirit requires a different, receptive movement. Remember, your guide has chosen you and you must let her spirit come to you as it will and allow your limbs be guided by the energies which swirl around you.

Many people use rattles which they shake rhythmically, whether dancing to call an animal, honor their own animal guide or discover her, but this is not necessary; you can dance to your own beat, which comes naturally to your body. Many shamanic practitioners recommend a preliminary starting dance to attract the attention of all animal spirits and evoke their sympathy.[6]

Dancing gently on the spot you might, for instance, begin summoning the animal spirits of the East, the direction of the rising sun's energy and life, while rattling quickly and decisively above your head, holding in your mind the images of oriental denizens such as Panda, Tiger, and Cobra. Moving in time to your rattles or just keeping a steady pace turn to the South, thinking of spirits such as Sloth, Jaguar, and Penguin. As you turn to the West, celebrate spirits from the great open plains such as Wolf and Bison; to the North, spirits of the ice – Polar Bear and Elk. Look to the skies and call to Bird, to Bat, and to Bee, and celebrate the wonder of the stars, the sun, and the moon. Then bending low, celebrate the seas and the creatures who live within them, Seal and Ray; the soil and the plants it nourishes, insects like Ant and Worm who toil within it, and the animals who make their homes within it, Fox and Badger.

Having sincerely honored all life and called upon the spirits, with your eyes half-closed let your body sway and move as you sense the eddying energies around you. Unthinking, let your feet move of their own accord and soon from the swirl around you one creature may become more distinct. You may visualize her or simply feel her in your soul. Perhaps it is Llama. Think of her nimble footsteps as she traverses rocky paths, consider her gentle, smiling disposition. Soon your feet will be following hers. If you feel the urge to cry and call like Llama, give form to your voice.

After three or four minutes, with sincerity ask your guide to stay with you to give you well-being and wisdom. Rattle loudly and let your feet take on random steps.

The dance is over.

GOING TO THE WILDERNESS:
VISION QUESTING

In North America in particular, future Shamans frequently retire to the open wilderness, remote caves, or other solitary places and, calling upon all their reserves of will, seek a vision of their animal spirit.

Cultures differ in their prescribed rituals. Some individuals retire for twenty-four hours, some for forty-eight hours, some for even longer. Some sleep so that their animal spirits may come to them in their dreams; some stay awake so that their perceptions become heightened, their connection with this reality more tenuous, making them more receptive and open to seeing their helping spirits. Some may eat, some may fast – their lowered blood sugar conducive to an alternative perception. Some drink copiously or take psychotropic drugs; others do not.

For those who come from a busy urban environment, just spending twelve daylight hours utterly alone with no sounds but those of nature is a very enervating experience. Hours spent in the dark without food or sleep heighten perception further; shapes form amongst the shadows and become real. Your guardian approaches, for your privations and heartfelt pleas that she reveal herself have touched her. Acknowledge her with joy.

It may also be that a flesh-and-blood representative of your animal spirit will appear if you are in her native environment. She, too, will make her presence obvious – Raven might swoop down and touch you with her wing, Squirrel might scurry to your feet. Greet them with joy.

Vision questing is not for everyone, and no one should undertake it without preparation. If you have never fasted before, going into the wilderness for two days with no food is a very bad idea indeed. And you should never attempt this without letting others know exactly where you are going.

JOURNEYING WITH YOUR GUARDIAN

Once you discovered which animal spirit or spirits have chosen to be your guardians and guides, you can call them to you before you enter non-ordinary reality. You may feel more relaxed having their benign presence by your side as you fly to the sky or make your way through your tunnel, knowing you will not be alone when you emerge into Shamanistic cosmology.

Devote your first few journeys to becoming friends with these magical creatures who can so enrich your life and imbue you with well-being in every way.

Let them explain their powers and their own desires, for if they have chosen you, they often have their own very specific reason. Once your relationship has begun to blossom you can begin to venture into this new geography guided by your spirit, and ask your guide to introduce you to other spirits and divinities. The geography you see and the spirits you meet are your own. There is no one journey – whatever you see is the reality that exists in tandem to this and may be very different from someone else's world.

You may now also wish to journey with specific aims. Many people journey to consult their animal spirits about problems or dilemmas they are facing on earth. When you first consult your spirit, ask questions that are simple to answer. As you begin to know your animal guide more intimately, you can ask her more complex questions and find her answers fruitful.

She may answer the questions herself or perhaps take you on a journey of discovery. All you need do is to be open to what is revealed, no matter how strange it appears.

DEEPENING YOUR RELATIONSHIP WITH YOUR ANIMAL GUIDE

Our animal guardians do not stay with us forever. Some come for a few years, some for a few months, but while they are with us they bring energy and well-being. Even when they are attached to us they become restless and travel, particularly while we sleep. This does not mean that the power they invest us with immediately disappears. Author Michael Harner believes that our power animal can be absent for up to two weeks before its positive effects on us begin to dwindle, and a sure sign that our power animal has gone for good is if we constantly wake in the night "depressed and dispirited".[7]

The more restless an animal spirit, the more likely it is to stray; the more tenuous its connection, the more likely it is to absent itself forever. Like any relationship, this is two-way. One of the reasons your animal spirit is with you is because she enjoys the experience of being in ordinary reality. And one of the ways in which you can let her experience this is by dancing (see page 28), having carefully observed the way she moves on earth, and imitating her way of being as faithfully as possible. Another way is to ask her to join you when you walk, particularly in a natural setting. Wolf might like to frisk by your side, Lizard walk ponderously, or Eagle fly overhead – what is important is that you keep their image in your mind and feel their being with you. Some individuals become their animal spirit, darting quickly like Fox, bounding like Gazelle – although if you choose to do this in a crowded park, be prepared for some curious glances. When you journey, you can make it your sole purpose to communicate with your guardian so that you both feel pleasure.

If you perform either of these honorings once a week you will renew the power of your animal spirit within you, making you feel generally healthier and more effective in dealing with day-to-day problems. Also, your animal spirit will be more content.

Read everything you can about her, understanding her natural way of living. If you possibly can, try at least once to see her in her natural habitat. If you are unable to – and we cannot all visit the Arctic to see Polar Bear, or the neo-tropical jungles of South America to see Sloth – do not visit her in a zoo. You can learn nothing from an eagle who cannot soar, an elephant who cannot live her complex family life, a rabbit who cannot burrow. These creatures are as dispirited as a human without their guardian, or a man serving a life sentence with no hope of release.

Keep a picture or a photograph of your guide in a pleasant place in your home, and perhaps make a sacred space for it. And do what you can for her earthly incarnations. If your animal spirit is endangered on earth, join organizations dedicated to her survival. If she is hunted mercilessly for "fun", join those who protest against this. If like Squirrel she lives in your garden, leave her a handful of nuts when you can. The more honored your animal spirit feels, the longer she is likely to stay.

DIVINATION AND UNDERSTANDING ANIMAL MESSAGES ON EARTH

A Lapland Shaman in a trance state divines the future

During initiation, Shamans learn the secret language they will use to communicate with their animal guardians, usually from an elder Shaman, and sometimes from the spirits themselves. Very often this language originates in the cries and sounds of earthly animals, and many Shamans also learn to imitate the voices of the animals around them. In the 1930s one anthropologist noted that a Kirgiz-Tatar Shaman, while springing, leaping, and roaring around his tent "barks like a dog, sniffs at the audience, lows like an ox, bellows, cries, bleats like a lamb, grunts like a pig, whinnies, coos imitating with remarkable accuracy the cries of animals the songs of birds, the sound of flight."[8] Besides helping the Shaman tune into these animal powers, throughout the world knowing the language of animals and especially of birds is the equivalent of knowing the secrets of nature, and hence being able to soothsay. These animals can reveal the secrets humankind so longs for because they are the earthly manifestations of divine beings. Learning their language allows communication with alternative reality, which is the source of all things that happen here. Like journeying, it is another way to communicate with the beyond.

Here on earth, this means that the greater your understanding of animal languages, the more easily you will be able to interpret messages from any animal spirits who wish to communicate with you, and to some degree anticipate what may be happening in your future and sometimes the future of others. We hear the sounds of creatures that surround us and those we see on wildlife programs, but do we really *listen* to them? Have we ever taken the time to actually interpret what they mean? Have we ever considered the other myriad ways they communicate with different behavior patterns, touch, and smell? Crow cries, Tiger roars, and Cat meows, but their vocal language is far more complex than this. For Cat, "meow" is the principle building block of her language, capable of myriad variations in emphasis, pace, delivery, quality, volume, and repetition. If you are a Cat devotee then almost without your realizing it, Cat will have trained you to respond to a host of non-vocal cues. Sitting by the door is a clear request for you to open it. If you fail she will utter her usual "meow" appropriate for this request and, confident that you will comply, will put a "heavy stress emphasis on the initial vowel of the vowel pattern."[9] If you still do not do as Cat wishes, she complains bitterly by stressing the first syllable of this particular "meow", becoming louder with every repetition. Once you can speak Cat you can understand a huge variety of messages she may wish to give you, and the same goes for every other creature.

The Animal Wisdoms in this book give a key to explain what the special presence of any animal spirit means to you. You can, however, if you wish use this as a foundation to gaining even greater insight into their wisdom and observation is the key. Start with the creatures that are easy to observe, the ones that have opportunistically taken advantage of urban life such as Squirrel, Fox, Raccoon, and Mouse and those who live in parks such as Deer, Swan, or Bat.

Concentrate on one animal spirit's language at a time and keep a journal of your observations, noting what sounds they make and behaviors they employ, and try to understand their meaning. Imagine, for instance, that Squirrel has made her presence obvious to you in a dream, or by unusually coming in through your kitchen window. It seems she may have a message for you. When you next see her in the park, she is chasing another squirrel wildly up trees and across open grass. What do you think this means? You might interpret this as aggression and flight, but in fact it is part of Squirrel's courting ritual. What does this mean to you? If you have been thinking of asking someone on a date, Squirrel is telling you to be bold. If you didn't know Squirrel's language, you could never have interpreted her wisdom.

It is also worthwhile noting if a particular animal behaves in a specific way when you approach her and what happens in your life in the twenty-four hours after you saw her. Perhaps every time you walk past Crow she caws once loudly and struts away – are there parallels in your own life? Every time Crow does this, does a particular type of event happen in your life – is there a synchronicity? Is Crow warning you of something, for instance, or trying to make you take an opportunity?

The wisdom of the animals is infinite, and they let us share in it freely with compassion and love. Accept their gift with gratitude, and join the cosmic dance.

PART TWO

DICTIONARY

OF

ANIMALS

THE ANIMALS

ANT

TOGETHERNESS · INVENTION · PURPOSE

ANTS HAVE populated the world for over fifty million years. Their kingdoms occupy jungle, desert, forest, veldt, and dune; sidewalks, houses, planes, and boats. They may be in the earth below or the trees above; they dwell in tunneled cities and silken nests, and traverse the ground as nomads. Architects and weavers, thieves and fighters, hunters, farmers, and gatherers of sweet aphid juices and dry seeds, Ant works from what she has, creating curious, useful beauty. Ant adapts, and so must you.

Ant as your guide shows that you may be the architect of your own reality, the creator of your own dream, but you must grasp the opportunities that life gives you and work with them. Some people spend their whole life waiting for a better or a different opportunity. Ant tells you that if you seize the day and work persistently with what you have, you will be rewarded. She also teaches that we are part of an interdependent whole, that nothing may be achieved in isolation, that the cleaner is as vital as the surgeon.

The queen and her lover mate while flying wildly through the air. Fecund with over a hundred million sperm, she returns to earth and rips off her wings, sacrificing flight that a kingdom may be born in which every ant plays a crucial role. Tiny workers care for fungus gardens, larger ants harvest leaf fragments to nourish the fungus, while great ants, who would crush the gardens, patrol and protect. The kingdom flourishes. Colony members greet one another by exchanging regurgitated food and glandular secretions that convey messages, such as if a queen is present or the type of food currently available. Within thirty hours the news has spread throughout the kingdom. Co-operation and social cohesion is all.

Your Ant guide counsels that you work closely with others, sharing your hopes, inspirations, and ideas for the good of the whole, be that your immediate family or the world. This way your own success, emotionally and materially, will be secured.

ARMADILLO

DEFENSE OVERCOMES AGGRESSION

ONLY TEN THOUSAND YEARS ago Armadillo, larger than Hippopotamus, trotted on giant claws across the open plains of Patagonia. Smaller now, her name in human language means "little armored one". She fossicks still.

Giant Armadillo is a formidable digger, clawing her way into the base of Termite's many chambered, rock-hard castles, creating great underground tunnels. Glands in her long pointed mouth secrete a thick glue with which she coats her long, snake-like tongue – one hundred termites are hers in a single nutritious lick. If Armadillo has moved slowly across your dreamscape, it is time to dig beneath surface appearance. Presume nothing until you have examined the situation carefully. Many believe that if Dog is large and boisterous, she must be vicious – but if they knew her better they would realize that she is simply playful and wants to be their friend. Likewise, see behind the hard exterior of Armadillo to something worthwhile within.

Armadillo is all about defense. Three-banded Armadillo's plating is so perfect that she curls into an impenetrable sphere sealed by triangular shields on head and tail, which form a curved rectangle. When danger threatens she has no need to flee nor fight. Her living fortress is flawless in design. Knowing this, she can stay for long periods of time on the earth, a virtually indestructible breathing coconut.

As your guide Armadillo counsels that running from confrontation, like fighting aggressively, is exhausting. If you set firm, defensive boundaries, the words and actions of others will slip away unnoticed as the claws and teeth of those who would try to attack three-banded Armadillo slide off her shields, unable to gain purchase. Armadillo advises that the time has come to defend your space. If you are always the one who pays for the coffees or is always called upon to drive friends to the airport, calmly make it clear that those days are over. Soon people will stop taking advantage of you and your integral territory – mental and physical – will once more be your own.

ASS

INTELLIGENCE · STRENGTH OF WILL · HELPFULNESS

Sɪxᴛʏ ᴍɪʟʟɪᴏɴ ʏᴇᴀʀs ᴀɢᴏ Dawn-Horse browsed only the forest, but her descendants branched out onto grassy plains. Two million years ago various species of superbly adapted *Equus* evolved, including Horse, Zebra, and gentle African Ass, the ancestor of domestic Donkey.

Ass is known for her stubbornness, but Ass is far from stubborn. She is extremely intelligent and, unlike Horse, possesses a mind of her own. She simply refuses to carry out tasks that might endanger her, such as descending precipitous paths of loose crumbling shale which might easily give way. If Ass has patiently walked by your side as you journey or dream, ask yourself if you are doing things other people want you to do that deplete your well-being, be that physical, mental, or ethical. Ass counsels that you too stay strong and refuse to do that which goes against your grain. We all have the right to politely say no to anything we wish – from not eating factory-farmed chicken, even if it has been cooked by our mother-in-law, or dangerous sports if they frighten us.

Yet Ass is the most helpful of creatures. She often stands head-to-tail with a friend, resting her head on the other's warm furry back or looking gently over her shoulder. When her friend's head is down, it enables sweet Ass to swish away swarming, iridescent Fly, who so plagues the eyes of all Ass spirits, with her long, coarse-haired tail. When both creatures have their heads up, the entire panorama of their environment is covered and any threat immediately discerned to mutual benefit.

Ass has always been there to help humankind carry its weighty physical burdens uncomplainingly. Jesus rode into Jerusalem on Ass, alluding to reaching places spiritual and physical that cannot be reached without assistance. As your animal guide, Ass advises you that it is now time to help other people – your friends, your partner, or the endangered animal spirits of the world. Like Ass, you will find that your help returns to you by way of karma, and that benefits you cannot yet imagine will accrue in your life.

BABOON

COMPANIONSHIP · PASSION · COMMUNICATION

INCOMPARABLE BABOON has many guises. In the great plains of the Savannah he is modestly brindled and displays a bright pink rump; in the somber forests of West Africa the thick flesh below his penetrating eyes is scarlet and electric blue, his beard a deep orange. High in the mountains of Ethiopia a fabulous cape of fur, long and golden, drapes his back, and a heart of scarlet flesh adorns his chest. Why so exotic, so vivid, so varied? To satisfy feminine desire.

Baboon has her favorites and certain predilections, to which her female offspring also incline. A penchant for fluorescent lilac buttocks edged with purple has become fixed and exaggerated in the male line because it is to these averred favorites, with whom she sits in companionable silence and grooms attentively, that she ardently offers herself when fertile. Baboon shows his delight in the earlier signs of affection by mating with her above all others, keeping her safe from attack and, if needed, munificently acting as a "godfather" to her offspring, even if fathered by another.

Sublime Baboon, adept of love, asks you to muse on the dynamics of your own romantic relationships. Have you been taking your partner for granted? Baboon changes his very flesh to please his consort. It is time to consider what you may do to please yours and, like Baboon, celebrate the sexual essence that makes your relationship special, and appreciate the balance of yin and yang which, through difference, makes a harmonious whole.

Baboon wears her heart confidently upon her sleeve, her desires unmistakable. Baboon counsels that you too open your heart to your loved one. If your partner is unsure of your emotions and your intentions they will be reluctant to show theirs; fertile ground for tragic misunderstandings. Baboon does not pretend. Her passions and shows of affection are genuine, her reactions without artifice. Baboon's wisdom is that of truthful, heartfelt communication and open expression of feelings. Be like Baboon, and you will find true and lasting love.

BADGER

COURAGE · AGGRESSIVE DEFENSE · PLAYFULNESS

Bold Badger fears none. Disdaining camouflage, she wears her audacious black-and-white livery confidently – a badge of her courage, warning others that she is a fierce adversary who will not hesitate to retaliate. She

readily dispatches those who ignore her warning with crushingly powerful jaws and the ripping strength of long foreclaws, while snarling furiously and exuding a noxious smell designed to frustrate her enemy. Badger gains further psychological strength from the security and tradition of her ancestral underground homes, which can be hundreds of years old. Labyrinthine in design, at crucial junctions it contains chambers large enough only for Badger. This allows her to easily defend the warren of rooms and tunnels beyond – the residence of her extended family – from any foolish enough to breach her citadel.

If Badger has dug her way into your life, the time has come to throw trepidation and fear aside, to abandon compromise and the dissembling which leads to defeat. She counsels that you take a firm, unwavering stand and speak your mind, regardless of what others may think. Fight valiantly, openly, and aggressively for those things and people you believe in, for that which you love, be it a fellow human or a forest, and for what you need in life – for if you do not, you now risk losing them forever.

Terrible and determined as Badger can be to those who would threaten her, her heart remains playful. When Badger's cubs emerge from their set, gamboling and frolicking is on their mind. How joyously they chase one another in the warm sunlight, yikkering and squealing, before engaging in a bout of wrestling or leapfrog, and Badger joins in. As your guide she reminds you of the value of play, how it will relax your body and release mental tension allowing you to deal readily with fraught, confrontational situations. As a cub, play gave Badger the skills she needs to defend her world, and as an adult it assures her continued prowess – just as it will yours.

BAT

TRANSCENDENCE · REBIRTH · LISTENING INTENTLY

Bᴀᴛ ꜰʟɪᴇꜱ ᴛʜʀᴏᴜɢʜ limitless night, swooping, turning, and twisting, traveling high at as much as sixty-five miles per hour (105 km/h). But Bat has not always had this unbounded freedom. Once Bat scurried on the ground, a small mammal, with tiny webbed forefeet devouring earth-bound insects. But Bat saw the skies with their plenty and used her forefeet to glide as she leaped into the air. Time passed, and Bat still strove for the sky until forefeet became winged hands and Bat, miraculously, really could fly.

If Bat has chosen to guide you, you are truly blessed, for she knows that you hold within the ability to become anything you want, but you must partake of her wisdom for your dream to take form. Everything has its own period of gestation and as you progress to your own limitless future you must transcend failure and its attendant fear, that of striving again. Instead make the knowledge it brings your own effloresce, and repeat the process until, on the destined day, you are reborn. Bat finds warmth and security by mingling companionably in the caves and luxuriant foliage that are her home. Emulate her and, as you strive, find comfort in friendship.

When Bat stretched her wings in the air she possessed abilities and senses unknown to her former self. Bat can send sound as a pressure wave through the air and react to its echo in six-millionths of a second. She can sense the slow crawl of a juicy caterpillar or an infinitesimal insect fifty feet (15 m) away, invisible on a faraway leaf. She advises that you, too, stretch your senses. Spirits you may be dimly aware of could be whispering magical secrets to you. It is time to seek quiet places and listen to the wind as it rustles through the trees to hear the messages it brings.

Be open, and let the words take form. Bat also counsels that you hearken to the words of those around you and the hidden, rather than the overt, messages that hey hold.

CONSERVATION · TIMING · NURTURING CREATIVITY

BEAUTIFUL, BRAVE BEAST, Bear is the true spirit of the wilderness which, without her and wise Wolf, would wither to a denatured park and in so doing take something vital and alive from our very souls. Twenty-thousand square miles of wild tundra (52,000 sq km), rugged mountains, teeming rivers, and dark forests are the massive home range of brown Bear. Hefty, intelligent Bear needs space to roam, to be free and untrammelled as she gathers mellow berries, nuts, and herbs, pounces on rodents, and fishes for the oil-yielding deep-pink salmon which endow her with vitality and the rich life-giving fat she needs to winter in her snow-covered den. Bear calls to the untamed heart of us all.

As your guide, she counsels that the time has come to strengthen your connection with wild nature, to open the channels to the world that exist without the city and suburb's invisible boundaries. Immerse yourself in the wonders of Bear's domain and flourish. Help conserve it for your children, and Gaia will flourish. This is Bear's wisdom.

Bear mates in the fecund warmth of summer but her tiny embryos remain in limbo, unattached to the nutrient-rich blood supply of her uterus wall, waiting for Bear to determine the correct moment for their growth to begin. Bear knows her reserves of fat must be deep to sustain their development and to furnish them with milk through winter, so she will not give life to her fleshly creations unless she can provide for them. Bear knows that timing and preparation are all, and advises that you too deliberate carefully before bringing anything into being. If Bear judges her situation to be auspicious, in spring she emerges from her earthy, secure haven with new life – her cubs – and searches for the forest's gift of vitalizing, luscious honey. Bear counsels that you also nurture your creativity by withdrawal, whether in meditation or retreat. When you return to the material world your ideas will bear fleshy ripe fruits, and you will again discover the sweetness life offers you.

BEAVER

ENERGY CONSERVATION · FAMILY · SECURITY

Glossy, brown-furred Beaver creates her water-based domain from land's bounty: munificent trees. Skilfully she engineers a dam, from sticks, rocks, and logs, and then her winter lodge. Roofed with woven twigs whose tasty leaves and bark Beaver has already eaten, plastered with muddy debris which in winter freezes to make the den impenetrable, and with its only door deep under water, Beaver may rest safely within. Finally she assembles her underwater larders of plaited branches and sticks to sustain her until spring, when the ice that seals her watery empire melts. Beaver's wood-chiselling teeth can fell mighty trees four feet (1.2 m) in diameter, their canopies laden with lush food and ideal building materials, but for Beaver, biggest is not necessarily best. Her wisdom is energy conservation.

Dragging branches across land offers predators opportunity and is a hard harvest indeed. Steering them deftly through the water that takes their weight is a far easier task. No matter how temptingly ample and luxuriant a tree, she reaps it only if it lies within forty yards (36 m) of her watery sphere, and usually only if it grows on its edge. After Beaver has removed large trees, sun-loving pioneers willow and aspen populate the clearing. These lesser growths Beaver can coppice year after year – a truly sustainable harvest – and effortlessly tow to her lodge.

If Beaver has come to you now, consider your own energy consumption. Are you taking on projects that are far too large and which sap your effectiveness, your vigor, to leave you vulnerable? Are you squandering your body's vitality by rising early, retiring late, and eating fast food? Are you wasting precious irreplaceable natural resources? Beaver counsels conservation, with all its meanings and in all its forms.

Beaver's intricately constructed lodge is more than a house, it is a family home providing succor and protection. She mates monogamously for life and keeps her offspring safe until the call of the wild bids them leave. This archetypal family unit still haunts our dreams even though our lives may be very different. Beaver's lesson is that you turn longing into reality and transform love into life.

RESPONSIBLE PRODUCTIVITY · PLAY

Flowers patiently await life-giving, humming Honey Bee. Their glorious petals, yellow, blue, purple, and ultraviolet, nod gently in the balmy breeze of summer. Their fragrances, delicate and heady but all exquisite, drift on the air with only one purpose: to lure Bee and ensure their reproduction. Her reward is their sweet nectar, which she transforms to honey, ambrosia of the gods and man, and her sustenance through the cold months of winter; and pollen, which nourishes her larval young. Without busy Bee, who pollinates the overwhelming majority of flowering plants, whose rich produce of fruit, vegetable, and seed provides for man, beast, and bird, the world's ecosystems would decay and the web of life itself unravel.

Bee is simply one of the most powerful creatures on earth. None of us is insignificant in the vast schema we inhabit, and Bee counsels that whatever you do or, just as importantly don't, do in life makes a difference that is positive or negative. You have the power to keep the ecosystems of the world healthy by recycling rubbish and buying food that has been grown without the use of pesticides which decimate Bee, Beetle, Butterfly and Ant, or to pollute and degenerate them. Your power is infinite. If Bee has come to you now, she is asking you to look within and see how you use it: wisely, for the good of all? Or thoughtlessly, making the world, and ultimately your own life, something far less than it might otherwise be?

When Bee discovers a carpet of flowers heavy with nectar she flies back to the hive to perform her bewitching waggle dance, whose orientation and speed directs other hive members to the blossom's exact location. She then gathers the nectar which she stores in her own body and, laden with bright yellow pollen piled in the baskets on her legs, returns to the hive, sometimes having visited over a thousand flowers. Bee works hard, but this messenger reminds you that her honey makes warm intoxicating mead, and that a life without frolic and fun lacks sweetness.

BISON

ABUNDANCE · THE RICHES OF THE PAST · ENDURANCE

Monolithic Bison, magnificent wild lord of the grassland prairies, embodies strength and endurance. Her matted woolly undercoat and thick, rich brown shaggy coat allowed Bison to range far into the unforgiving Northwest Territories and survive the Ice Age, which brought about the extinction of so many other mighty mammals. The tracks of her once tremendous migrations can today still be seen from the air, a testament to her enduring presence.

Her multi-chambered digestive system ferments the coarse low-nutrient grasses on which Bison dines and transforms them into heath-giving vitamins and sustaining energy. Much biotechnology, regarded as the cutting-edge of science, is based on this very same process – as is the production of so many staples of our lives: bread, cheese, beer, and yogurt.

The wellspring of creativity and personal growth has its basis in the past. Bison counsels that the time has come for you to draw upon its riches. For some, this may involve looking into their family tree, discovering the multicultural roots that make them the unique individual they are today, and blossoming to their full potential. For others, it could mean being like ancient alchemists, transmuting the old and seemingly worthless to a vibrant new form, or rediscovering fabulous lost processes or wisdom.

If Bison has come to you now she signals that the time for abundance is coming, but you must be prepared to recognize its gifts and its form, physically and spiritually. Bison once sustained the Plains Indians, giving them the flesh of her body for food, her fur for warmth, her hide for shelter. In recognition of her great sacrifice, no part of her being was either wasted or squandered. Bison counsels that abundance is not about a consumerist materialism that denudes the earth of irreplaceable resources in order to provide transient objects, but the plenty that comes from walking in harmony with creatures, plants, and insects, respecting the very minerals, ores, and soils from which the earth is fashioned.

BLACK PANTHER

THE FEMININE · SEXUAL POWER · SENSUALITY

Black as the velvet night under whose auspices she hunts, Panther moves silkily, silently, softly, on great strong paws. The ultimate ambush predator, Panther pounces so swiftly and so expeditiously that her quarry has no intimation of her coming until it is captured and carried off to her arboreal lair. Like Black Panther, be stealthy in all your dealings. Let no one know of your intentions until the time has come for action, or all advantage is lost, be it in love or in business. Panther counsels also that you make neither empty promises nor empty threats, which will only divest you of your power and leave you lost.

Black Panther is rare and mystical. Mistress of the waxing and waning moon, she is the puissant symbol of the feminine in its many guises: mother, virgin, seductress, Amazon, soothsayer. If Panther has chosen to guide you, she is giving you the opportunity to balance the masculine and feminine forces within your psyche and to awaken powers and passions that may have been dormant since birth. It is the most masculine of men who can nurture their children, and the most feminine of women who can engage in combat, for both accept the totality of their beings.

Icon of sensuality and fundamental sexual energies, Panther moves lithely – smooth muscles rippling under sleek glossy fur. She lies languorously on warm, high branches, her long tail flicking lazily as a reminder of the might coiled within, waiting for release. Who does not desire to run their hand slowly down her warm luxuriant flank, to look deep within her dark magnetic eyes to discover the myriad secrets that lie within? But who dares?

Panther challenges you to accept your own intrinsic sexuality, whose true force and nature you alone know. Society, rejection, the expectations of family, and scars carried from abusive relationships can cause this vital and intrinsic part of our humanity to shrivel or find outlet in other forms. Panther advises you that the time has now come to reclaim your sexuality and sensuousness, and to embrace life. For some this may be a tough path to walk, but with Panther padding beside you, anything is possible.

BOAR

TO YOURSELF BE TRUE • THE POWER OF TOUCH

BOAR IS A SPIRIT of such unparalleled intelligence, ferocity, strength, and fearlessness that even Tiger, absolute ruler of the Eastern jungles, must treat him with respect; for Boar reverses the traditional roles of predator and prey, frequently leaving Tiger mortally wounded. For those whom Boar has chosen to guide, the wisdom of Tiger will also say much.

The lore of the jungle casts meaty Boar as a banquet for others, but Boar proves tradition wrong. As your animal guide, Boar counsels that you should not allow society or other individuals to dictate the part you play in life. Constant friction between outer persona and inner desire causes stress, deep unhappiness, and, with time, coruscating resentment. If the role you perform is a sham then your relationships with others will also be false. Be true to yourself so that you may in turn be true to others.

Earthy Boar relishes the physical. When resting, he lies touching another rotund, comforting body and greets through touch – either nose-to-sensitive nose or nose-to-mouth. Grooming with great incisors and disc-like nose bonds him to others. Mutual massage using responsive snouts gives sensual pleasure and keeps muscles supple. Boar understands the continuum of body and mind, that an unhappy body makes for a tense or restless mind. Boar knows the power of touch.

Those whom Boar has come to in their journeying will benefit greatly from restorative therapies, such as Ayuvedic massage. And as Boar has a highly developed sense of smell, aromatherapy massage will be wonderfully beneficial, as will time invested in learning about the therapeutic powers of flowers, barks, and particularly the roots, tubers, and grasses so beloved by Boar.

Boar also knows of the secret power of music, and courts his chosen female with a bewitching *chant de coeur*, or love song – a serenade of rhythmic grunts so potent that it induces her to mate with him. Music can uplift the soul, cause torrents of tears, or engender anxiety, calm, and passion in turn. As the body can heal the mind, so the mind may heal the hurt within the body. This is the true wisdom of Boar.

BOWER BIRD

ATTRACTING LOVE • CREATING A WELCOMING HOME

Bower Bird LIVES in the evolutionary young and deliciously lush land of New Guinea, the land formed only ten million years ago from the extravagant eruptions of underwater volcanoes. Male Bower Bird, like most feathered males, must make strenuous efforts to attract a mate and pass on his genes to the next generation.

New Guinea is an earthly paradise for Bower Bird. Inhabited by neither Monkey nor Squirrel, who would eat of the fruits, flowers, nuts, and seeds of the forest, nor even medium-sized predators such as Weasel, means that male Bower Bird has an unparalleled opportunity to express his worthiness. Vogelkop Gardener, a type of Bower Bird, builds a complexly woven hut large enough for even man to crawl into and at its entrance displays his tempting collections of treasures, arranged according to their persuasion: a pile of shiny black beetle wings, a mound of delicious plump red fruits, a collection of bright-pink petals, and shining orange leaves. He must work hard to maintain his showcase and guard it carefully lest others steal its most gorgeous gems. Withered fruits and moldy petals must be excised, new pleasing items added every day, and his collection rearranged to best advantage – each an individual work of art.

Female Bower Bird tours the forest bowers inspecting their architects' work. When she finds a hut that truly inspires her, she at last allows male Bower Bird to mate with her beside or inside his wondrous palace.

As your feathered guide, Bower Bird counsels that you too take care of your home and make it a beautiful and welcoming place. Do your windows sparkle, your houseplants flourish, are your sofas warm and deep, do candles magically spread sweet perfume in the air? Or do heaps of dirty laundry lie in a trail, knocked over coffee cups lurk beside chairs, and the smell of cigarette smoke pervade every nook?

Like Bower Bird, if you wish to find love you must prove yourself worthy. If your would-be partner adores olives, freesias, cigars, provide them in plenty – it shows you care for how they feel. Let your home be harmonious and friendly and the one you love will surely visit again.

BUSH BABY

INTUITION · PROBLEM-SOLVING · SIGHT

Bush Baby, five-ounce replica of the world's
first primate, has been leaping prodigiously
through the star-lit rain forests of Africa for sixty-
five million years. As dusk approaches, Bush Baby
leaves the comfort of her leafy nest and the
comfortable bodies of her kin, stretches, yawns,
and prepares to meet the night. Truly nocturnal,
Bush Baby detects the arrival of dawn before
humankind or their light-meter technology, and
returns home.

Only one-hundredth of the night's ambient light penetrates
her arboreal domain, yet Bush Baby can jump fifteen feet (5
m) horizontally and drop twenty-five feet (8 m) with
absolute accuracy. Her immense, round orange eyes with
their great reflecting layer see through 250 degrees, while her
head, like Owl's, moves through 180. Nothing escapes Bush
Baby's perception and no predator can catch her: Allen's Bush Baby
travels forty feet (12 m) in five seconds, pausing a mere twenty-fifth of a second
between takeoff and landing. Her long fingers, with their widened, flattened tips,
ensure her grip on even the widest of trunks.

If Bush Baby has leapt securely into your world, night and its mysterious feminine
energies must now be of paramount importance. Like Bush Baby you will be at your
strongest during the hours of darkness and also at your most perceptive and
intuitive. Walk in the silver light of a full moon or under the navy blue velvet of a
heavy sky and let your mind open – the solutions to problems will reveal themselves
with extraordinary clarity. Relax and look into the darkness, the shapes that form
in the shimmering, moving air amongst the shadows of trees and plants will answer
many questions.

What you see is now more important than what you hear. When talking with a
lover, a friend, a deal maker, or a business colleague, look deep into their eyes and
carefully observe the expressions that flit across their faces for that is where you will
discover the truth. Should you detect danger, an unfaithful partner, or a deceitful
deal, like Bush Baby flee with all possible speed, sure in the knowledge that you will
land securely.

BUTTERFLY

TRANSFORMATION · TENACITY · COMPASSION

Butterfly tastes flowers as she dances on their delicate petals, her glorious colored wings shimmering in the rays of a warm sun but her extraordinary beauty, gentleness, and seeming fragility belie her tenacity and bravery. Some, dauntless, scale the snowy alps to reach Europe, while others traverse the untamed oceans. Butterfly as your totem shows that openheartedness and compassion are not signs of weakness but of strength, and she counsels that through kindness and tenderness you will attain your goals.

Butterfly has a wider visual range than any other living creature. Her ability to see ultraviolet light means she sees designs and colors invisible to mere mortals. As your guide she suggests that you cultivate the invisible powers of telepathy, of extra-sensory perception in all its richness, so that you may see and understand what others do not, and the patterns of your life and those of others may be revealed. The color most attractive to Butterfly is yellow, so if she has chosen you as her apprentice make sure that yellow features in your environment and know that its appearance in your life has meaning.

Butterfly is also the spirit of dancing transformation and utter joyous metamorphosis. From egg comes the caterpillar who, when fat and plump, sheds her skin to reveal a jelly-like mass that hardens to becomes an impermeable pupa. From this seemingly dead mummy emerges Butterfly, her bright wings crumpled, soft, and drooping. Within moments her body fills their cells with life-giving liquid and imperceptibly they strengthen and open. Poised, now ready to journey, she takes to the azure skies. Beauty has been born.

Butterfly shows that to resist change is to remain forever unformed, soft, and squashy, or mentally crystallized, performing meaningless ritual and empty habits, closed from the greater whole. Her guidance is that even the most radical and transmuting change is natural, and to embrace change is to perform an effortless dance to the rhythm of life, bringing you through time to reach your creative, emotional, and spiritual potential and utter fulfillment.

CAMEL

TRAVEL · ABANDONING THE KNOWN

INCOMPARABLE DESERT DENIZEN, Camel travels where others simply dare not venture. She evolved fifty million years ago in North America and once roamed the lands that are now Los Angeles browsing on sage. Moving north and west over the then extant land-bridge to Asia, she continued to flourish there after the great extinctions. Nomadic Bedouins domesticated her and named her Ata Allah, or God's Gift, because in her bounty she blessed them with shade against the blazing sun, creamy, sweet nutritious milk, wool for garments, and dung for fire-fuel. Sacrificing her own body for meat and hides, Camel was the Bedouin's magical carpet who flew them across the burning, glistening sands.

Camel's nose seals tightly to keep out sand while her beautiful, large soft eyes are protected by a double row of luxuriant lashes. Great two-toed, webbed feet allow her to cross soft sand without sinking, and she can find nourishment in the desert's thorniest scrub and driest vegetation. Camel stores her energy as fat in the humps on her back and is able to convert it to water through oxidation – she can allow the temperature of her body to rise and so not lose precious water through sweat. Remarkably, Camel can survive two months without water and then drink up to thirty gallons (114 l).

If Camel has swayed majestically into your dreams, consider where you might journey – physically and mentally. Camel knows that it is time for you to seek new landscapes, even if, like the desert, they at first seem harsh and foreboding. But desert sands in the wide full moon are a most beautiful shimmering vision, an oasis a magical confection laden with dates and good things. As Camel's body conformation protects her, within her humps carrying what she needs to traverse the sands, so you carry within your mind the knowledge and strength of will to go anywhere you choose – nirvana, another dimension, the wind-swept Russian steppes. It is time to leave the safe and familiar to discover the wonders that the world holds in store for you. Camel will guide you safely.

CAPYBARA

IILLUSION · THE MAGIC OF WATER · GENTLENESS

Capybara lives in the southern Americas, in some places a wild garden of Eden. Gaia's heaviest rodent at one-hundred and thirty-two pounds (60 kg), Capybara's solid squat build and large, sharp, chisel-like front teeth belie her sweet and inoffensive disposition revealed so plainly in her gentle, dark eyes.

Seventeenth-century Catholic missionaries hungry during Lent wrote to their supreme leader of a creature "scaly but also hairy" – Capybara has tough skin and sparse hard hair – who "spends time in the water but occasionally comes on land" and asked if it might be classified as fish. The church concluded that indeed it was fish, and so might be eaten during Lent – a resolution that stands to this day, unfortunately for Capybara.

If Capybara has lazily wandered through your dreams, it is a reminder that things are frequently not what they seem. Did you see your new paramour kiss someone goodbye with affection, and feel overcome with jealousy? Make sure it wasn't a brother, a sister, or a grown-up offspring before leaping to conclusions. Intuitions and intimations of telepathic communications can lead you astray. Capybara counsels that you should devote yourself to the factual and not let fancy hold sway. Fool's gold glistens brightly, causing many to toil and mine laboriously for no reward. Think very carefully before investing time or money lest your goal be maya, mere illusion.

Capybara ambles nonchalantly across the great prairies of which she is mistress before taking to the river to float blissfully amongst great crowds of purple-flowered water hyacinths. For water is Capybara's sanctuary – she hides beneath its forgiving surface to evade Jaguar and man, makes love in its warm currents just before the onset of the rains, and sleeps within it securely, only a protruding warm brown nose betraying her presence. Capybara knows that you too can benefit from contact with this most nourishing of elements. Sitting on the banks of a river listening to the murmur of its rush or swimming easily in the open air will relax your body and soothe your soul.

CAT

ADAPTABILITY · REMAINING TRUE TO YOUR SOUL

Urban jungle, suburban sprawl, and rural idyll alike are Cat's empire. Sinuous, sensuous queen of all she surveys, she lives with us but is not ours. True always to her essential being, cat has never been domesticated – she is simply the consummate mistress of the pre-eminent skill of survival: adaptability. As she lazes luxuriously on our silken cushions and carefully licks our offerings of cream, seemingly so gentle, so ultimately content, her heart dreams of the coming night when bathed by the light of the mystic moon she again becomes the huntress, sacred to ancient powerful gods, to Diana, to Isis, to Artemis.

In the farmlands of Europe and the great spaces of America, her feral self dines on nourishing Mouse and relishes Rat; in the crowded squares of great cities she blends seamlessly into the light and dark dapples of her world, accepting the bounty humans heap upon her but never forgetting she is what she is. Cat is as essentially feline as her wild relatives, the jungle cat, the leopard cat, the rust-spotted cat.

As your guide, Cat counsels that you too stay true to your own nature, no matter what the vicissitudes or largesse fate brings, or the flattery or criticism of others. With equal alacrity, Cat climbs ornate velvet drapes in million-dollar apartments or the crumbling wrecks of derelict tenement blocks, flourishing wherever she finds herself. Sometimes, no matter how great our strength, how puissant our will, we cannot change our circumstances. Cat advises that you do not waste precious energy on fruitless endeavor, nor spend time wondering what might have been, but examine your situation impartially as a stranger might. Cat knows that there is always another way, that within the most difficult situation the seeds for advantage wait to be fertilized.

Cat sees far into the night. Glittering and incandescent, her crescent-moon pupils become full; she observes the material, ethereal, and mystical alike. Cat counsels that you too trust to your senses, to the hunch that comes unbidden, to the message that appears in your dream – and follow your destiny.

CHAMELEON

EXTRA-SENSORY PERCEPTION · PATIENT AMBITION

FANTASTIC IN HER DESIGN, Chameleon at once combines extraordinary beauty with the exquisitely bizarre. Chameleon fascinates. Chameleon bewitches. And so may you, by accepting yourself as you are. Chameleon is at one with herself and her world, her senses subtle, artful, otherworldly. Seemingly spellbound, she moves purposefully, deliberately along the branches and twigs that form the highways and paths of her leafy arboreal home, while wondrously the hue of her dry warm body varies continuously, mimicking the colors that surround her. Chameleon's very skin senses her environment.

If she has chosen to guide you, it is time to become aware of the diffuse rare energies that surround you and that you, too, possess – the senses beyond taste, touch, smell, sight, and sound: the aura of others, psychic communications from afar, the etheric vibrations that emanate from us all – and to study their meanings and essence. Trust to these senses, because they are real. Remember that just as the colors of Chameleon's world change, so the energies, emotions, and desires of those around you remain in constant flux, and to flourish you must adapt to them. But Chameleon is not always dull greens and nondescript browns. When she wishes to warn off an intruder her display is vivid and colorful; when relaxed, a light leaf-green. Others need to know how you feel, too.

Chameleon dines on succulent insects. An incomparable ambush predator, she waits motionless, invisible, for her hapless prey to land nearby, independently swivelling turret-mounted eyes and keeping ever-attentive watch. The insect settles. Eyes lock swiftly on her target, giving its accurate depth and location. Chameleon's sticky-tipped tongue, longer than her whole body, unfurls and takes her quarry in less than one-hundredth of a second.

Chameleon brings the wisdom of biding your time quietly in the tricky worlds of commerce, work, or politics. Become gray and unnoticeable, a ghost in the machine, perfectly positioned to seize opportunity until you have assessed the myriad currents and independent ambitions in the situation – and only then, like Chameleon, make your move.

CHEETAH

SPEED IN DECISION-MAKING • PLURALITY

Cheetah, fastest-living mammal, flies through tawny, dry Savannah. Delicate, long-limbed frame coated with ever-rippling, supple muscle, unsheathed claws spiking the hard ground, her hind paws reach between fore paws with ever-increasing speed. Cheetah's eyes lock on her twisting, turning prey as she sprints at seventy miles per hour (112 km/h). A feline in canine formation, Cheetah stalks silently with cat wisdom through low rugged rocks, behind spired termite palaces and thorny bush, belly held low, mind alert, chasing her quarry, the fleet gazelle, with all the power of sight-hound magic.

Cheetah is truly exceptional. What other creature partakes of two natures? Look inside yourself to discover different talents and ways of being. Forget crystallized patterns and rigid monoculture. When ponds are dry and rivers cracking mud, Cheetah survives on fat green watermelons, their pink crisp interiors swollen with moisture from months of accretion. Celebrate the plurality within your soul and the many ways of bringing it to the world, for Cheetah is offering you the chance to be exceptional, too.

Black tear-stains mark the tawny fur of her neat triangular head from ear to mouth. Does Cheetah mourn that she has sacrificed the strength that big cats know for the delicate body that makes her vulnerable to Lion, Vulture, and Hyena, yet which bestows upon her such speed? No, for Cheetah knows the value of camouflage, alliance, and co-operation. Irregular dark shapes spot her creamy body rendering her invisible, while in coalition with others, male Cheetah enjoys the rich bounty of prime hunting territory. Cheetah chooses not to walk alone, and profits. Remember this wisdom, lest others stronger or wilier take that which is yours. Consult Lion, Vulture, and Hyena, for they too have lessons to teach you.

If Cheetah guides you, the time to hesitate is over. Decision followed by resolute action is imperative. You dwell on the threshold, but you may stay there no longer. As Cheetah grasps her prey, so you must grasp what life offers.

COBRA

TRANSFORMATION • DEEP SEXUAL ENERGY

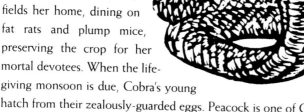

INCOMPARABLE SNAKE, charismatic and magnetic, Cobra's dual powers of creation and death make her irresistible. An object of intense cultic worship, Cobra knows her land's deep primordial secrets. When an abundant rice harvest is due Cobra makes the paddy fields her home, dining on fat rats and plump mice, preserving the crop for her mortal devotees. When the life-giving monsoon is due, Cobra's young hatch from their zealously-guarded eggs. Peacock is one of Cobra's few enemies, and those whom Cobra has chosen to guide should consult the wisdom of Peacock also.

Guardian of water and savior of grain, the very staples of life itself, Cobra counsels that you consider your fundamental needs from which flow all creativity and vitality. Feed your body with energized whole foods, be they flesh or fruit, and walk amongst nature. Change and rebirth is inevitable, and strength is required. She advises that you embrace the inevitable, even if it appears undesirable. Although things seem worrying, as Cobra sheds her old skin so will you be shedding everything that has been holding you back.

Cobra's eyes take on a trance-like milky cast as she prepares for transformation and she counsels that you, too, meditate on the meaning of change and the path you wish to follow. As her skin sloughs, Cobra's eyes again clear. The future is revealed to her as it now will be to you. Cobra's energy lies coiled in the base of your spine, and she waits for you to loosen it. Sexual and alluring in form, Cobra raises her head sensuously in invitation to her mate who moves sinuously over her body, entwining it with his before finally copulating. In salutation to this puissant energy, she is living guardian of the sacred phallic lingam in the temples of Shiva, Hindu god of creation and destruction. Cobra counsels that sexual energy is powerful and should not be given lightly, but that when given freely in mutual respect and love it is a true alchemy. She suggests you look carefully at the meaning of desire before letting this energy free.

COYOTE

CURIOSITY · INTERTWINING LOVE

Intelligent, curious, and canny, Coyote has been celebrated in Native American culture for over ten thousand years. European settlers have always persecuted her, but she persists and diversifies. No part of North America is now without this sharp-eyed spirit – like humanity, she proliferates.

Coyote is clever, Coyote is ingenious, Coyote is crafty and observant, full of power. Coyote is serious for he must survive, but he is playful and sensuous too. The ancient Aztecs depicted him as the god of pleasure and hedonism; to many indigenous North American peoples, he is the joker and the trickster whose tricks sometimes backfire on him. Yet the divine Fool, personified in the tarot, holds within him the wisdom of life and is poised to step into a new future. Coyote's behavior holds a mirror to our own as in him we see ourselves, reflected with all our so human dichotomies of spirit. Magnanimous and mean, sacred and profane, wise and foolish, we make our way.

If Coyote has chosen to trot beside you on sure paws, he has come to warn you not to take yourself or your plans too seriously. If by being pompous and self-righteous you lose the ability to laugh at yourself life will surely trip you up, making you the mundane fool, not the divine fool or seeker. It is time to laugh at your mistakes and the jokes the world plays on you, to do the crazy and chortle. Seeing things so differently allows a new wisdom and new way into your mind.

Coyote also understands the lessons of enduring love. He stays with his partner until death parts them, and in life spends eighty percent of his time in her company. She marks their territory by urinating, he lifts his leg on the same spot, a potent affirmation of their equality and the interwoven texture of their lives. They curl up together in the warming rays of an afternoon's sun and dine on Elk in harmony. As your guide, Coyote counsels that you, too, intertwine your life with your love's, acting as one – an inseparable unit – or risk love running away, leaving you alone, the foolish one.

CRAB

REGENERATION · COURAGE · THE RHYTHM OF NATURE

CRAB MAGICALLY MOVES to the rhythms of a mysterious opalescent moon, her whole being synchronized to the waxing and waning of this primeval orb. As the Moon controls the tides of oceans and seas, so Crab lives in tune with their high and low tides, the phases of the Moon and her rising and setting. The hatching of her tiny free-swimming larvae coincides with the high Spring tide so that they may populate far-away sands and rocky pools. True to her lunar goddess, Crab conducts the rituals of her busy life nocturnally.

If Crab has chosen to visit you as you dream, the rhythms of the celestial bodies influence you profoundly and are more important for your well-being than you yet know. Crab counsels that you align your life with nature. Become aware of the circadian rhythms that influence hormones and other biological mechanisms of your being, rise with the life-affirming Sun, and sleep under the aegis of the mystical Moon so that you may truly thrive.

Crab fears few attackers. Her soft body is armored by a rigid carapace, and she has stout pincers with which to defend herself. Should her opponent grapple with a leg or hold on firmly to a pincer she breaks free leaving the appendage behind, for Crab knows the secrets of renewal. When the rhythms of the heavens accord, Crab begins to grow a thick wrinkled "skin" beneath her carapace. When her preparations are complete she molts, leaving herself intensely vulnerable, but now capable of regeneration and growth. First she absorbs water into her body, stretching her skin until it is too large for her normal body, and miraculously replaces missing limbs. Over a period of two-to-three weeks she hardens her shell and finally gradually grows to fit her new tough armor. Crab bids that you protect yourself from harm but counsels that with the courage that allows risks – be they mental, or the physical trials implicit in many sports – comes immense spiritual and emotional growth.

CRANE

WISDOM • JOY • PEACE

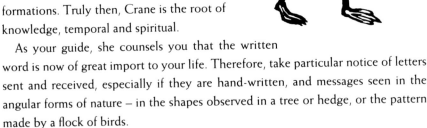

SPECTACULAR IN HER long-legged elegance,
Crane flies high through Asian skies of
azure blue, trumpeting and calling. A
mystical messenger of wisdom, in legend
she flew to other worlds and carried
venerable Taoist sages on her long, strong
back. Some believe that the first alphabet was
formed by a Cretan man, Mercury, from the
chevrons and angles of her group flight
formations. Truly then, Crane is the root of
knowledge, temporal and spiritual.

As your guide, she counsels you that the written
word is now of great import to your life. Therefore, take particular notice of letters
sent and received, especially if they are hand-written, and messages seen in the
angular forms of nature – in the shapes observed in a tree or hedge, or the pattern
made by a flock of birds.

Crane is also a winged emissary of peace. Legend tells that in eleventh-century
Japan a feudal leader released hundreds of her kind as a thanksgiving for the
victorious end of battle and the beginning of concord – each with a prayer for those
slaughtered attached to her leg. Crane counsels that it is time to end enmity with
neighbors and those we once loved, and to join with all humanity in giving peace,
not war, a chance.

In the sumptuous wetlands that are her home, Crane dances magically. Her
fluttering love-steps are a complex and intricate courtship studded with great leaps
of joy and passion, the throwing of feathers and beauteous stones in the air.
Sometimes she dances simply in happiness when she lands after the arduous journey
from her winter domain, or when her chick, fledged at last, makes its first flight.

If Crane has danced before you it is now time to celebrate the wonders of everyday
life. In contemporary times birthdays are often disregarded, Christmas an hysterical
buying frenzy. Crane advises that you celebrate friendship, a beloved pet, another
year of your own extraordinary existence – for we are all truly unique – doing the
thing that you love the best, be it drinking champagne or walking under a gibbous
moon. Like Crane, allow yourself to see the joy in life and flood your being
with happiness.

CROCODILE

PRIMORDIAL KNOWLEDGE · THE FRAGILITY OF LIFE

GUARDIAN OF THE margins between land and water, of the mud from which life springs, Crocodile's spirit haunts the invisible plane between life and death, the eternal cycles of destruction and birth, and as such is the keeper of all knowledge. Silently slipping through her riverine world, Crocodile waits patiently for the unwary deer or chattering monkey to drink carelessly at her borders. She snaps and twists. Death has again yielded life.

On the banks of the mighty Brahmaputra and the sacred Ganges, Gharial Crocodile lays her twenty eggs and buries them in the protective sand of their shores. She guards her creation carefully for sixty days, while the early warmth of a Sun more ancient than even she incubates the life within, but still the shadow of death passes over them. If Crocodile's babies hatch while still buried they will suffocate and die; if she takes them from their sandy womb too soon they are a feast for another. While still safe within their shells her babies, when ready to breath the air of earth, cry out – loudly, recklessly – causing Crocodile to race to their side and excavate them. Her miniature replicas then cut themselves free. Crocodile gently puts her children between that mighty weapon, her fearsome jaws, and takes them to the river's edge. There with other babies they learn the secrets of Crocodilian life, while a consortium of mothers guards their crèche.

Crocodile is cold-blooded and must bask on propitiously positioned rocks and sandy banks to take the sun's energy and make it her own, storing it in the very heart of her body. Without its power she could neither survive when temperatures dipped nor be able to digest the great chunks of flesh she had consumed. Crocodile's wisdom speaks both of the enduring nature of life and its utter fragility, of gentleness and ferocity, of care and neglect, and of how all energy is ultimately transformed. If Crocodile has chosen to guide you, the time has come to examine the primordial mysteries of life and prepare yourself for miraculous rebirth and the wonders it will bring.

DEER

SOLIDARITY · GENTLE ACTION · CO–OPERATION

HIND – GENTLE, ALERT, every sense keen – stands motionless amongst the leafy trees. The dappled light falling on her irregularly spotted body renders her invisible until a delicate ear twitches in response to a sound deep within the forest, or her nose crinkles in recognition of a familiar scent. If Deer has revealed herself to you now, be especially aware of what drifts to you on the breeze. A snippet of conversation, the fresh spice of cologne, may hold secrets untold.

Hind has no defense against mighty predators except for the premonition of danger, which enables her to flee; to find safety she and her doe-eyed fawns, those sweetest of creatures, gregariously gather with others of her kind. Her wisdom is that of pacific solidarity. A peaceful protest, such as boycotting the goods of an unethical company, goes unnoticed when performed alone. Performed by thousands, it can bring a corporation to its knees. If Hind has chosen to guide you, it is time to again be at one with the groups to which you belong, or seek to be part of a bigger whole. If you are estranged from family or friends, Hind counsels that the sagacious and secure ask for forgiveness and forgive in turn, offering a place of repose for mutual love and the regeneration it brings. Sometimes this can be a hard wisdom to bear, but if Hind has chosen to guide you she will help you to find the gentle strength you need.

Deer also knows the wisdom of co-existence with other creatures who are quite different from herself. Langur, long-tailed monkey of the Indian forest, feasts greedily on fruits high in tropical trees. Deer waits patiently for Langur to drop her bounty, so that each benefits; and together from their separate vantage points they are better able to spy predators, be they Tiger or man, and may warn each other. The combining of diversity creates harmony and stability. Embrace kindly those whose lifestyles are at variance with yours, and reap the rich rewards.

DOLPHIN

PURPOSEFUL CHANGE · RETURNING TO OUR ROOTS

PLAYFUL, SLEEK SWIMMER, gregarious, intelligent mammal of tropical river and deep ocean, no creature has adapted more elegantly to her world than Dolphin. Sixty million years ago her thickly furred four-legged forebears bestrode the earth. Fifty million years ago in swamp and marsh their metamorphosis began, with the slow elongation of body and the gradual disappearance of hind legs and fur to form a body so streamlined it could move through water at twenty-four miles per hour (38 km/h).

Dolphin embodies the power of patience and as your totem shows how with time and slow determination, which celebrates change little by little, you can create wonders, move mountains, and become the person your heart desires.

The element of water seems to provide everything that Dolphin needs, but as she moves rhythmically through the white-crested waves she remains wedded to her origins on earth. She must breathe the salty air as she breaks through the water's surface and is unable to resist riding the bow waves of human ships in joyful acknowledgment of her primordial, land-based self. She reminds you never to forget your cultural and familial roots, to seek them out and celebrate their diversity and richness by including their fruit in what you create today.

Dolphin also shows that breathing is more than just a means of supplying oxygen to the body but a tool which may be used to heal body and soul, awaken sexuality, and induce altered states of consciousness. For those whom Dolphin guides, practicing breathing techniques will be especially beneficial, allowing you to journey deeply into the worlds below.

Dolphin schools and orca pods are the wolf-packs of the deep. As one they repel their predatory enemy, the shark, help injured and disabled companions, and hunt in intelligent co-operation. Orcas move resolutely along the coast, herding giant schools of salmon together and finally encircling them tightly. They then, in turn, lest the salmon escape, feast on the nutritious oily flesh. Synergy is all. Dolphin teaches that the whole is so much more than the sum of its individuals.

DRAGON

POWER IN BALANCE · CONSERVATION

DRAGON, ANCIENT MAJESTIC lord of the waters, is also fire-breathing and capable of flight on mighty wings of leathered skin. Truly, Dragon is the very incarnation of the four elements of Gaia: fire, earth, air, and water. Partner of White Tiger, yang to her yin, azure Dragon also represents the balance of masculine and feminine, of darkness and light, and the procreative powers of sexuality.

Dragon is long gone from our earth. Some would say that she never existed at all but there are those whose great-grandparents say she still stalked the remote areas of mystical Transylvania two hundred years ago, but was persecuted to extinction. Recently discovered German fossils, now known as archaeopteryx, show unlikely flying creatures with great talons at the end of their wings – something Swan still possesses – long bony lizard-like tails and bony jaws full of teeth. Pterodactyls once beat their wings above primeval forests. Scales and feathers are both constructed with horny material and originate as tiny pouches in the skin, the evolution from one to the other certainly possible. Who can ever really claim to know the truth? Archaeological remains are sparse indeed and the inner biological functions of these ancient creatures, in many cases, simply unknowable. Is it our rationalist inability to believe that any flesh-and-blood creature can breathe fire, which makes us doubt that Dragon ever walked the earth or soared in its cavernous skies? And yet he is recorded time and again in societies from Wales to China. What is certain is that he lives on powerfully and vibrantly in all the cultures of the Old World – another species of flying creature discovered in 1995 has been named Chinese dragon-bird — and is now making inroads into the New.

Dragon is in the mythology of all our minds and he is there to remind us to preserve the fabulous and diverse forms that surround us still. He asks that Tiger, his consort through eternity, is not robbed of the lands that are her birthright, that her fantastic self is not obliterated in order to make dull rugs and quack medicines. He asks that we give all creatures the respect and wild space to live that has always, until now, been there. Dragon is relying upon us.

DRAGONFLY/DAMSELFLY

WARM LOVE · PROTECTING WHAT IS YOURS

DRAGONFLY, IRIDESCENT gossamer-winged being, sparkles vividly in hazy sunlight reflected from lucent pools and streams. Did this mighty dragon of the skies ever walk the earth and scorch it with her fire? Journey to her world and seek sincerely of her wisdom, for she can surely tell you tales of ancient wonders far beyond the power of dreams.

On this orb at least, Dragonfly moves between the realms of water and air, symbolic of the deep pull of emotion and the rational clarity of intellect. Her larvae develop in lakes, marshes, and rivers: the speed of their transformation to glittering, colorful maturity is dependent upon the surrounding warmth and richness of the food supply. Damselfly larvae in the north take two years to emerge, but in the balmy, bountiful south, just four months. Once in the air, Dragonfly is a decisive, soaring predator. Dining on Frog, Spider, Bee, and Termite, Dragonfly zealously protects the territory where his mate will deposit her eggs.

If Dragonfly has danced into your life, it is time to consider the balance between your emotional well-being and your rationality. All creatures, children, and romantic relationships that are nourished with warm emotion and care flourish. Your rational mind may say that it is ludicrous to waste time walking in the woods at twilight with your partner when you need to do the ironing, but your rational mind is wrong. Without the positive expression of love your relationship will shrivel and, like Damselfly's larvae stranded in cold icy water, die. The laundry, on the other hand, will still be there tomorrow.

Perhaps your childhood was unhappy, forcing you to hide your emotions behind an intellectual facade. Dragonfly counsels that the time has come to examine those issues, even taking professional assistance if necessary, and let light and color back into your life.

Your emotional mindset may tell you that it is right to play the doormat, acceding to every unreasonable whim your partner voices, and always to put them first. Like Dragonfly patrolling his territory, you must always protect yourself appropriately, and strive for balance at all times. Equilibrium, then, is everything. This is the wisdom of Dragonfly.

EAGLE

KARMA · VISION · RESPONSIBILITY

MAJESTIC EAGLE inspires all those who see her. A traveler between worlds, her powerful wings take her soaring to the Sun, allowing her to ride upon the winds, rise on the warming air of morning, and to plummet to the earth to grasp her prey in unforgiving, razor-sharp talons. Eagle's deadly weapons can kill Monkey with one hard blow, and she is the only predator who can take Sloth from her leafy retreat. Therefore, those whom Eagle has chosen to guide should also consult the wisdom of Sloth.

Eagle is the mistress of feint when hunting, and ruthless when she strikes. Eagle, however, only kills out of necessity. She uses her powers neither for malice nor spite. There are times when we all need to be ruthless in business and in our personal lives in order to survive. Eagle, however, counsels that before striking you consider carefully the effects of your actions and whether they are truly justified. The deal that takes what little another possesses to increase your own wealth for the sake of greed can have repercussions far beyond the immediate – and not just for others.

As your guide, Eagle gives you the power of vision and the ability to penetrate the mysteries of other worlds and then return to your own, but it is you who must develop the discipline required to achieve this.

Eagle regularly fishes for her food, often diving down into the water from a height of several hundred feet before returning to air, her natural element. She sees Rabbit, hopping toward her burrow for safety a mile into the distance; from a thousand feet up (304 m) her sharp yellow eyes identify prey over an area of almost three square miles (7.8 sq km) but the vision she gives to you stretches through time, from the deep past through the fluctuating present and into the myriad realms of the future.

Use this power wisely to develop your spirituality, your creativity, and your healing abilities, for your karma will come as swiftly as Eagle's flight, and its outcome for good or evil is firmly within your hands.

EEL

ENCHANTMENT · ENIGMA · EXPECT THE UNEXPECTED

Eel, MYSTERIOUS INHABITANT of fresh and salt water, is conceived in the great swirl of ocean currents and undulating seaweed of the far Sargasso Sea, yet grows to golden maturity in the sylvan-banked rivers of England. Does your legendary home of Atlantis still lie in Sargasso's green-blue depths? Does your spirit yearn for its lost sanctuary?

Eel embodies mystery, magic, legend, and transformation. If she has swum snakelike through your dreams, be prepared for enchantment and enigma in any form. Expect the unexpected, and question nothing.

When Eel leaves the Sargasso she is less than two inches (5 cm) in length, a tiny creature who hitches on the Gulf Stream for three years until she reaches Europe and England's Severn River. She migrates up rivers, she piles with ten thousand of her kind so that those at the top may reach the smallest of creeks; she slithers through wet grass and burrows through soil, as nothing stops Eel reaching her destination. She grows to maturity and the years pass by, until one summer's night when the call of Atlantis is overwhelming. Eel migrates downriver through the Baltic. Her once-golden body transmutes in mysterious alchemy to silver, rendering her almost invisible in the ocean's swell. Her eyes grow and their pigment changes so she may better see in her new world and finally her very gut dissolves. She must reach her destiny three thousand miles (5,000 km) away on energy stored, then spawn and die. Or perhaps she morphs into a being unknown, or dissolves in the silvery sky, for humankind has yet to discover the secrets of Eel.

Eel speaks of many things: of the ability to change absolutely, of the power of alchemy, and becoming something so clearly unlike what we were, so that like Eel we become unrecognizable. To be what we must is the ultimate, fundamental state of our being, and this is the moment to embrace it.

Eel tells also of the power and the pull of place. If your heart yearns for Paris, for Esfahan, for Samarkand, Anchorage, or Bombay and you know not why, fly there with the speed of light and, like Eel, meet with your destiny.

ELEPHANT

FAMILY LOVE • AGE BRINGS WISDOM • ALTRUISM

ELEPHANT, IN MISTY TIMES gone by, lived in languid rivers and cool limpid pools. Although she now makes the land her home, Elephant still returns daily to the original source of her being to drink deeply of its life force: to bathe, to roll, to wallow, and swim in the warm tropical waters of the Bay of Bengal. A mighty colossus who bestrides the earth on fleshly pillars, Elephant is also the embodiment of sentience, heart-felt emotion, altruism, and maternal love, which may endure for fifty years.

Her calves find shelter from the blazing Sun when she pushes them beneath her great stomach and with her strong trunk lifts them to safety from raging flood waters, even at the risk of being swept away herself. When drought strikes, to keep her calf cool she sprays it with water regurgitated from her own stomach. With her trunk, so little different from a human hand, she holds on to her tiny calf's tail and when older, her calf will clasp hers as they amble togethr from place to place.

A matriarch whose experience and wisdom is respected leads Elephant's close-knit family group, sometimes for many decades. It is she who decides when it is time to cease foraging, to rest for the night, to visit the dark caves where mineral-rich salts lie, and she who in times of danger gives the command for group defense, retreat, or open attack. Should she be shot her family, rather than desert her, surround her sadly and frantically, risking their own lives. If she has fallen injured they lift her to her feet and walk her to safety, supporting her bulk on their trunks.

If Elephant has chosen to walk by your side in your journeying, she seeks to speak to you of the unconditional love that only your family gives unreservedly. In times of trouble we sometimes turn away from our families, even our mothers. Elephant counsels that the time has come to accept their love and, like Elephant, learn from the wisdom accrued over a lifetime.

FLAMINGO

LIFE GIVES BEAUTY · FLOURISHING IN ADVERSITY

Beautiful, flamboyant, flaming pink Flamingo lives in one of the most hostile environments on earth: the baking volcanic salt lakes of the African Rift Valley. As the heat rises through the summer, Flamingo's lake evaporates, concentrating its briny salts, and at Lake Magadi, salts of carbon and sulphur solidify to become caustic white curds. But Flamingo has developed scaly feet and legs to protect her, and webbed toes prevent her from sinking into the viscous gummy mud beneath. And what is harsh for one is manna for another – algae and brine shrimp proliferate wildly, providing Flamingo with an abundant supply of food and giving her feathers their glorious, flashing color. So wondrous did the ancient Egyptians consider the scarlet flush of Flamingo's plumage that their hieroglyph for red was a silhouette of her exquisite form. But the color fades in feathers taken from her living flesh, a reminder that true beauty is intrinsic to the living and that the iridescent wings of a butterfly, feather, and fur stripped from the dead lack magical energy and their power to transform.

Flamingo possesses the most complex beak and tongue of any bird. They allow her to filter around five-and-a-quarter gallons (20 l) of water a day, separating salts from the microscopic plant life that nourishes her. Truly she is a mistress of discrimination. As your guide, she counsels that you too should examine all offers and information which now come to you with the utmost care. Not everything nurtures and, like Flamingo, you must sift from your life that which is harmful.

If Flamingo has dramatically swooped into your journeying, she comes with a lesson for survival. Flamingo's world is harsh, dire, and unforgiving, but she flourishes and in the end is made even more beautiful by it. As your guide, Flamingo counsels you that no matter how appalling circumstances beyond your control seem, no matter how devastating a tragedy, there really is a way of dealing with it. Flamingo could not banish the burning salts nor bid the sun flame less fiercely, but Flamingo did not give up. And now she is right by your side to offer you her blazing strength.

FOX

OBSERVATION · UNDERSTANDING OPPORTUNITY

CAPTIVATING FOX, bewitching and beguiling: now you see her, now you don't. Was she ever really there? Fox, mistress of camouflage, patrols the Arctic in livery of snowy white. In the northern Americas the rustling, inviting branches of trees cloak her pelage of gray and rust, while in cities unforgiving and hard, Fox, quick and russet, melts seamlessly into the ever-twilight night. Magic must surely be in the air.

Fox tells of the wisdom of stillness and stealth and of observing unseen so that much may be learned and gained. Fox dines on blueberries and luscious grapes in season, ambushes tasty mice and jumping frogs, takes leaping fat grasshoppers and newly-laid eggs, feasts on offerings from kindly humans, scavenges hamburgers and chicken nuggets and the leavings of those who can take greater prey, like Wolf. For Fox is the supreme opportunist.

Every day holds within its core infinite potential for change. Every day brings new opportunities, if only we are aware enough to see them and brave enough to take them. Fox embraces opportunity and flourishes. When her territory is taken by humans she moves into theirs; when a fleet snake crosses her path, she swiftly pounces. Fox knows that opportunity waits neither for her nor for you. The snake is gone, the territory ceded to another. You may look at glass and see only its cool transparent surface, or look through to a world of myriad chances. The choice is yours, for Fox's wisdom is that luck is simply the ability to see a break and take it.

As your guide, Fox counsels that it is time to hone your senses until they are as sharp as hers. Fox's keen eyes detect the merest movement of either predator or prey. Once you start being purposefully conscious and alert to what is happening in the world around you and feel the interconnectedness of life, not only will you begin to see the inevitable outcomes to certain situations, but you will begin to instinctively know when an invitation is an opportunity. Fox counsels that you take it.

FROG

ACCEPTANCE • GATHERING STRENGTH

W ATER, ESSENTIAL TO Frog, is the feminine cleansing element of creative transformation. Frog's fertilized eggs lie in a warm mass beneath its protective surface. Soon their cells divide, and the tadpole, so similar in form to the male creative form, absorbs oxygen released in bubbles formed by their movement. Soon limbs develop and gills are absorbed. Frog emerges from the water. Finally her masculine tail is absorbed into her body – a perfect synergy of masculine and feminine energy. Frog is perfect.

Mistress of diversity in movement, she jumps vivaciously and athletically through life. Frog literally walks on water. She leaps through the air at distances fifty times her body length. She swims strongly in pond and stream and leaps from branch to branch using webbed feet to glide. She saunters on earth, her legs moving in a smooth, diagonal pattern; she burrows into moist soil and strolls securely on the glossy undersides of tiny leaves.

If Frog has chosen to leap into your life, consider how you are making your way. Frog conforms seamlessly to her environment from the humid tropics to north of the Arctic Circle, from dry, arid Australia to lands of perpetual rain. She encases herself in an impermeable cocoon of hardened mucus to guard against dehydration in drought. At high altitude in cold water where oxygen is scarce, she has developed a baggy skin that absorbs oxygen directly into her body.

Frog counsels that your strategy now must be to adapt and survive. We rail against fate, shout our discontent out loud, and make strenuous efforts to change our destiny, but sometimes life moves inexorably on and we cannot change what is happening, try as we may. For now, it is wise to accept the inevitable and use your energy to maximize any possible advantage. Conserve your vigor instead of depleting it and grow strong in the face of adversity, all the better to influence events when opportunity does arise. Transformation comes through adaptation and the cleansing of energy negatively used. This is the wisdom of Frog.

GAZELLE

SPECIALIZATION · SPONTANEITY

GAZELLE, FLEET AND GRACEFUL denizen of the arid African plains, roamed through Kenya fourteen million years ago. Gazelle survived the great extinctions because she is the supreme tribal specialist. Water is rare in her hot dry lands, and to avoid losing it from her own body she can raise her temperature by up to 10 degrees centigrade (50 degrees F) and has grown a light but dense coat to reflect the sun's burning rays. A grazer, Gazelle is able to dine on the succulent water-storing leaves and tubers of trees and bushes whose roots reach deep into the earth for water when its surface is dry, its grass parched. Nomadic, sometimes migratory, when one opportunity has been exploited she moves swiftly to another. So fast, so supple that even Cheetah can rarely catch her, Gazelle fears none. Curious and intelligent, she approaches the unknown and even the known predator with confidence, knowing that she can outrun them should danger threaten.

If Gazelle has bounded into your dreamscape, it is time to move on. Gazelle does not tarry in unproductive lands. If your job has given you all it can, your partner no longer feeds your heart and soul, your neighborhood feels tired and worn, like Gazelle leave them behind. You have no need to be fearful about the future, for if danger or difficulty threatens, like Gazelle make your move with lightning speed and discover that new opportunity beckons. Action is everything. Gazelle's horns which, unlike those of Deer stay with her for life, represent higher psychic powers. Even if you are unaware of this ability, you will instinctively find abundance because of it.

Gazelle's fawn is born on the plains. Unable to run, she is intensely vulnerable to predators. For the first weeks of her life the fawn has no smell, and lies hidden, completely still, and always some distance away from Gazelle – her existence is only evident when Gazelle calls her to suckle. Fawn is secret and safe. Like Gazelle, give others no intimation of your plans or, like predators destroying a fawn, they may be ambushed. Simply strike.

GIRAFFE

ADMITTING REALITY • RENEWING DISTANT TIES

Tallest of all creatures that walk the earth, uniquely marked with irregular chestnut-brown patches and blotches, Giraffe ambles lazily through her savanna homeland, grazing on the foliage of the beautiful bloomed but fearsomely thorned Acacia tree. Many find prickly Acacia too hard a dinner, but Giraffe's long tongue curls dexterously around its leaves, her lips and tongue protected from harm by horny papillae. From her lofty eighteen feet (5.5 m), the acute vision of Giraffe's large dark eyes reaches to the far-distant hazy horizon and sees what others cannot. Her colorful perception is acute, her premonitions strong. She sees the rains as they move inexorably toward her, dust rising in the distance. And none predates Giraffe.

If she has galloped into your dreams take great notice of the context in which this occurred, for it is sure to have some symbolic or literal reference to coming events. If she has now chosen to guide you, it is time for you to consider your own future – to look ahead and anticipate what may be coming for good or bad. Sometimes we know that something distressing is likely to happen, but refuse to admit to it. We anticipate an opportunity but cast that from our minds, too nervous that it may mean change or frightened that we may fail. Giraffe is aware and, because of this, is strong. Giraffe takes her leaves with skill and avoids harm. Expertise facilitates success, while self-knowledge imparts wisdom. Giraffe counsels that you look to the future with eyes as open and as large as hers so that you too may prosper and avoid adversity.

Giraffe connects with others who are at a distance, knowing the importance of unity and communication. She counsels that you too keep in touch with those far away. Because you do not see someone in your day-to-day life does not mean that they are not important – perhaps they have a message, an opportunity, an inspiration. Giraffe advises that it is time to renew communication with those in both distant lands and neighboring villages, and be amazed at what transpires.

GOOSE

AWARENESS OF TREACHERY · CONSTANT TIES

Magnificent feathered savior of ancient Rome, Goose was once an incomparable sentinel sacred to Juno, imperious goddess. All of Rome had fallen to the Gauls save the lofty Capitol citidel where Marcus Manilus and his men still held on. The Gauls, espying a hidden path, crept up by night to deliver the final blow. But Goose, alert in Juno's temple, cackled loudly and waddled weightily on strong yellow webbed feet to the troops. The Gauls were repelled, the tide turned and Rome was restored to its people.

As your guide, Goose counsels that you too should be alert to the secret machinations of those around you. Watch carefully how others behave, and with discretion, particularly when they are not conscious of your presence. Is there corruption at your workplace or in your local government? Expose it loudly. Has your friend been disloyal to you? Chastise them roundly. Ultimately victory will be yours.

Goose is one of the great migrating bird spirits nesting far from her winter home. As fall approaches she feeds on highly nutritious tubers storing energy in the form of fat, for Goose must fly non-stop, sometimes for over eighteen hundred miles (3,000 km) if she is moving from northern America to the Gulf. She waits for a following wind and warm airstream then, flying in "V" formation, she ascends to around four thousand feet (1,220 m) and cruises at forty miles per hour (65 km/h). In spring, fat again with luscious new grass shoots, she makes her way to her breeding grounds. Goose remains faithful even to her roost sites when she migrates. That way if her partner or group member gets blown off course, or lost in fog, they know where Goose will be waiting faithfully for them.

Goose counsels that you heed her constant loud honking as she begins her own journeying, and see in it an invitation to move to other realms and new dimensions, or to seize new opportunities. Like Goose, make sure you are prepared for your journey, physical or metaphorical, and having reached your destination remain faithful to it. For Goose knows that returning to the same spiritual truth, land, creation, study, or work, all of which possess complexities and depths that take a lifetime to unravel, will provide you with great fulfillment.

BECOMING GROUNDED · PROVIDING SANCTUARY

POCKET GOPHER, with her small ears and bright black eyes has not only colonized the United States but with Bison created its great grassland prairies. When Bison roamed wild and free, her voracious grazing denuded whole areas which were colonized by just those fragrant and nourishing plants Gopher prefers. The rise in volume of delicacies attracted Gopher, and soon her numbers multiplied exponentially.

Little six-inch (15-cm) Gopher, as she tunnels busily in search of delicious roots and tubers, moves a ton of soil every year greatly improving its texture, aeration, and water absorption. As she brought new mineral soil to the surface, it became mixed with Bison's dung and plant humus, and the deep loam beloved of America's great grasslands was created. Gopher literally shaped a nation.

But Gopher does more even than this. The mounds of soil she shovels so rapidly from her underground domain provide the perfect growing site for rare and beautiful plants, which need to colonize quickly and move on to avoid being overwhelmed by herbs and shrubs. Her burrows provide sanctuary for Salamander and Turtle, Rabbit and Skunk, and many creatures live only within her earthy network.

If Gopher has come into your journeyings, soil and its produce will heal and balance you. Organic gardening and all that it entails will inspire and ground you: the feeling of earth on your fingers; the nurturing of succulent vegetables, pulled from the damp ground and transformed into supper; the flowering of delicate blossoms whose fragrance drifts through your open window. Even the smallest of plots like Gopher's own domain becomes transformed into a habitat for myriad animal spirits from Bat to Butterfly, Fox to Hedgehog, bringing life and its calm vitality to you. Gopher counsels that if you feel nervous, wound up, hysterical, scattered, or are behaving like the proverbial space cadet, you need connection to the web of all life, and that there can be no more profound way of doing that than becoming a part of it. And this is the wisdom of Gopher.

GORILLA

EMPATHY · GENTLENESS IN STRENGTH

Gorilla, peaceable vegetarian of African lowland and the mountains of the Virunga volcanoes, truly is the gently giant of Gaia. He dines on giant celery, wild ginger, blackberries, and succulent herbs and, by disturbing the earth and its tiny tree seedlings as he does so, cultivates his land to produce more of his favorite nutritious foods. If Gorilla has gently walked with you as you journey, consider your own diet. Is your system sluggish? Do you suffer from indigestion? Do you dine on fast food and fizzy drinks? Gorilla counsels that it is time to cleanse your body – ginger is particularly effective – and feast on fruits and vegetables. Gorilla is powerful, awe-inspiring in his might – he is what he eats, and so are you.

Gorilla's emotions play over his expressive face: anger, fear, sorrow, surprise, and happiness. His great arm stretches out to comfort another, to offer reassurance, and he often mates face to face, looking into his partner's dark, liquid brown eyes. Female Gorilla stays constantly with her babies, who if left alone or separated from their mother wail pathetically in utter distress.

When Silverback Gorilla decisively leads his harem and offspring to forage, to find a new sleeping area, he considerately slows his pace if any member of his family group has been injured by the wire-snares of man, or is ill or suffering. He defends them to the last, from man and Leopard, sacrificing his own life if needs be. Yet Gorilla is truly terrified of man; if he has been hunted, the mere sight of a human being causes such extreme fear that Gorilla's bowels become liquid – so the courage shown by him and female Gorilla is truly exceptional, displaying a love that is transcendent.

As your animal guide, Gorilla asks you to meditate on the meaning of love, and to consider the expression of kindness. Think carefully as you ask yourself the following questions: Do you care for your family and friends as Gorilla does? Do they care for you? Would you sacrifice yourself for your mate? And would they sacrifice themselves for you? The answer to these questions will reveal with startling clarity the true nature of your relationships.

GRASSHOPPER/CRICKET

RELAXATION · SINGING YOUR LOVE

GRASSHOPPER IS THE harbinger of summer, her cheerful song trilling through meadow and field. More than that, Snowy Tree Cricket even broadcasts the warmth of a lazy humming day – add the number forty to the number of chirps she makes in a fifteen-second period for the temperature in degrees Fahrenheit.

Aesop's ancient fable tells that in icy winter starving Grasshopper asked Ant to share her seeds. Ant asked, why had Grasshopper not toiled to produce her own store? Grasshopper's reply was that she had been too busy singing. But what Aesop did not realize was that Grasshopper dies before the cold of winter, so she was far wiser than he knew to take delight in every day.

If Grasshopper has chosen to hop into your world, it is time for you too to relax and enjoy life. Work and worry are not always the answer. Like Grasshopper, bask in the rays of a kindly sun, draw energy from its beneficence, and think not of the morrow. For Grasshopper knows that when the time is right, like her, you will hop effortlessly into a waiting future.

Grasshopper rubs her back legs over special veins on her forewings, transforming herself into a living musical instrument. Male Mole Cricket amplifies his sweet tune by singing from a specially shaped burrow, which sends his song one-and-a-quarter miles (2 km) away into the balmy twilight. As your guide, Grasshopper counsels that you too send your song of love loudly to the one you adore lest they be charmed by another's mellifluous melody. Grasshopper performs enchanting duets with her love. Be like Grasshopper and listen to the heartfelt sounds others sending to you so you may embrace their emotion in harmony.

Music is intrinsic to Grasshopper and those whom she has chosen will find that playing a traditional non-electronic instrument – a simple flute, an acoustic guitar, a piano – will cause their entire being to resonate with the harmonics of the spheres, releasing their feelings and passions, bringing both peace and joy into their lives.

HARE

TRAVELING LIGHTLY · DISCERNMENT IN LOVE

Delicate Hare materializes from her mother's womb ready for life, her fur thick and soft, her gentle eyes open, her great sensitive ears twitching, her elongated back legs poised to make the leaps and bounds that will speed her away from predators. And Hare travels lightly. Unlike the hard and heavy carapace of other creatures, her skull has many hollows and her collarbone is small. Hare reminds you not to allow yourself to get bogged down with worries that keep you tethered to the present and tied to the past. What might have been and "What if?" are devoid of meaning, and serve only to prevent you from seeing your future. Hare knows that alone this can be a daunting task and counsels that group meditation or talking to another about your hopes and fears will help to clear, cleanse, and lighten your mind. You can then react quickly as the future speedily unfolds, both avoiding disaster and seizing opportunity.

As the first colorful flowers of spring carpet the grass and the Arctic bursts into lush life, joyous Hare begins the capering and boxing that leads finally to her mating. Standing on her powerful legs she boxes and cuffs her admiring suitors, testing their prowess and roundly despatching the hesitant. Male Hares who survive this rigorous trial must pit themselves against her in wild mad races and further tougher sparring matches to prove their suitability. Only then may the real leaping, jumping, airy courtship commence and its consummation, accompanied by squeaks and squeals of passion, take place.

Love is utterly overpowering. Infatuation sends us mad with desire and transforms the object of our affections into a divine being devoid of the flaws that afflict the rest of humanity – until our hormones calm and disillusionment sets in, or anguish pierces our very souls. Hare knows how fragile and easily broken are our hearts. If you are deeply drawn to another, take some time to look into their hearts and minds, to know their inner self, before you succumb to physical desire or hasty and absolute commitment. Discernment followed by passion leads to the magic of love. This is the wisdom of Hare.

HIPPOPOTAMUS

FRIENDSHIP BRINGS PROTECTION • NOURISHMENT

ONCE HIPPOPOTAMUS foraged for succulent grasses in ancient forests from Eurasia to Africa but as the millennia passed pacifically by, Hippopotamus abandoned her hard earth-bound existence for a life of ease in the world's mysterious fertile feminine rivers, emerging only in the cool of tropical nights to feed on their lushly carpeted banks.

Hippopotamus forges a close bond with her calves and protects them fiercely against other Hippopotami and any who would approach too near her fleshy treasure. The calves are perfectly adapted to nurse at Hippopotamus's rotund bountiful body while completely submerged in water, their tiny ears and wide nostrils automatically closing when they suck. The ancient Egyptians revered this mighty amphibious mammal they saw basking in the Nile as the source of all life, and deified her as the benign nourishing goddess Opet at whose breast the King of the Pyramid Texts asks that he may suckle so that he may "neither thirst nor hunger ... forever".

When Hippopotamus took to the rivers, she made sure that she could protect herself. Her eyes, ears, and nostrils all moved to the top of her massive wide-jawed head, allowing her to lie beneath the water's flow while keenly scanning her environment for any hint of trouble. A blood-like liquid exudes from the mucus glands in her vulnerable epidermis and, drying hard and shiny, safeguards Hippopotamus from dehydration, coruscating sunburn, and infection from cuts.

If Hippopotamus has swum strongly into your world, nourish those around you and be nourished in turn. On one level this involves the sharing of food – nothing creates bonds of friendship, love, and intimacy more easily than the sharing of home-cooked food in open-hearted hospitality. In a world of fast food eaten alone, Hippopotamus counsels that the time has come to again break bread with friends and family as humankind has done since the dawn of history, and to take succor from confidences given and revealed. Friends and family are eyes and ears looking out for us in a complex world and, like Hippopotamus's red-lacquer coat, shielding us from the vicissitudes of life. This is the simple wisdom of Hippopotamus.

HORSE

SPEAKING PASSION ALOUD · MALE SEXUAL ENERGY

PEGASUS, FABULOUS WINGED-HORSE born of Medusa, mortal incarnation of feminine wisdom, and fathered by Poseidon, deity of untameable seas and mighty waves, is the supreme embodiment of nobility, freedom and graceful fluid motion. Pegasus's mighty hooves thundered over earthly plains while on great snowy wings he could ascend even to the realms of the Gods. Immortalized, he floats in the heavens, a constellation of sparkling, shining stars. Horse is Pegasus returned to Gaia, the earth – as he trots and gallops for a moment his four hooves leave the soil, poised for flight, but he returns to earth so that humankind may continue to partake of his wisdom.

Unbounded, he canters through foaming white-crested waves of the French Camargue and dines on the sea's salt herbage in honor of his marine heritage – for who but a god might rule the oceans or tame wild stallion?

Horse gallops across Asian steppes effortlessly jumping river and fallen tree, his mane rippling in icy winds, his tail flying behind him, his steps a rhythmic poetry of line and form. Those whom Horse has chosen to guide will find their spirits and bodies set free in the magic of dance, and their whole sense of being transformed.

The epitome of virile male sexual energy, Stallion is lordly in his puissance. Quick to defend his harem from the attentions of others with awesome bites, he also uses this teeth more gently to herd his mares. His passions and intentions are openly declared, and strong at heart he knows no fear of others or of rejection. Like Stallion, use your mouth both to defend robustly those you love from those who would hurt or belittle them, and also let them know your feelings with ardent speech – for Horse knows that Cupid favors the brave.

Stormy Horse fights neither for territory nor dominance, but lives in free harmony on the wild plains. He respects others according to their age, and advises that you too respect your ancestors. Drink deeply of the knowledge that only a lifetime of living can bring.

HUMMING BIRD

CONSTANCY IN LOVE · THE MAGIC OF FLOWERS

Delicate iridescent beauty of balmy, sun-kissed climes, only Humming Bird, of all the feathered denizens of the skies, can float stationary in the air – a rainbow hanging before the blossoms whose nectar she sips. Humming Bird's wings beat twelve thousand times a minute, their tips wondrously describing the symbol of the infinite – an elongated figure of eight on its side – while creating heavenly sweet music. Music can transport us to other worlds and open us to a concerto of emotions, from deep sorrow to boundless joy. If Humming Bird has flown into your life, embrace music, let its magic open your heart and mind to love, wonder, and joy, so that you may experience the boundless, honeyed bliss that life can bring.

Humming Bird's slender dainty beak reaches deep into the tropical blooms from which she feeds, allowing her to harvest their bounty with her fine tongue. Humming Bird is faithful to the plants that sustain her so liberally – sword-billed Humming Bird drinks only from datura, Woodstar from hibiscus – and in doing so ensures their pollination and continued abundance in the world. Bee sips mainly from flowers of yellow and blue while Humming Bird almost always sups from those whose petals are red, the color we associate with love. Hummingbird knows that passion and devotion flourish and grow when hearts are constant, and that there is little more injurious to love and crushing to the spirit than infidelity. If a partner is unfaithful, it is time to soar away and taste the affection of another. If you no longer love exclusively, it is also time to fly away before you bruise another being and take away something essential from within your own soul that will leave you less open to love the next time it is offered to you.

Flowers are intrinsic to Humming Bird and will have great meaning for you, particularly if they are red. If Humming Bird has flown to you, you will find that surrounding yourself with blooms will lift your spirit, and creating a wildflower garden simply by scattering a few seeds will provide you with a restorative space that lightens your heart.

HYENA

SEIZING POWER · PHYSICAL FITNESS

GREAT CARNIVORE of African savanna, forest and plain, Hyena, magnificent in her power, will even best Panther. Her great head and massively muscled jaws contain teeth so robust that she can literally crush bone. Hyena and twenty of her comrades can devour a two-hundred-and-twenty-pound (100-kg) Wildebeest in its entirety in just thirteen minutes. Hyena's digestive system dissolves teeth and bones in a matter of hours.

Hyena roves her territories in great clans, and in this weighty society the lowest status female Hyena outranks every single male. Female Hyena has taken male energy and made it her own so completely that not only does she have a faux scrotum packed with fatty tissue, but her womb leads not into a vagina but a phallus as large as male Hyena's. When she becomes sexually mature the slit in her glans enlarges to around half an inch (15 mm), allowing male Hyena, after a diffident courtship, to mate with her and later her offspring to emerge. Eleven or more pounds (5 kg) larger than the male Hyena and often possessing considerably higher testosterone levels, the female Hyena is formidable indeed. And yet Hyena is the most diligent of mothers. Great strength combined with superior status to male Hyena means those in the top echelons have not only the choicest food, but more of it. As a result, Hyena's milk is nutritious and calcium-rich, and she can feed her cubs in one-and-a-half-hour sessions up to six times a day. Her cubs have not only the biological fitness but a social ranking that gives them the edge.

If Hyena has loped into your life as your animal guide, you must now claim power or remain weak forever. If you are female the time has now come to play men at their own game, to study masculine strategy, enact it decisively and win unequivocally. If you are male, you must call upon your solar masculine energies to the same end. No one cedes dominance, no one gives away power in any arena. It can only be earned with un-wavering determination, seized, and held. This is the wisdom of Hyena.

KANGAROO

Dark liquid eyes full of intelligence fringed with long lashes survey the vast wilderness that is Kangeroo's realm – endless plains surmounted by the vast blue dome of the southern sky – as she moves with prodigious hops up to thirty feet (9 m) long. Muscular, z-shaped legs propel Kangaroo forward at speeds of up to forty-three miles per hour (70 km/h), her mighty tail providing balance and ballast. Kangaroo burns energy quickly when first she begins to hop, but once her rhythm is set, her energy seems to replenish itself as she bounds tirelessly under a warm sun.

Kangaroo and her relatives know no obstacles, no bounds. Rock Wallaby inhabits cliffs, springing from ledge to ledge, and can leap up even the sheerest of rock faces. Kangaroo is simply incapable of moving backwards – she knows only how to progress.

If Kangaroo has hopped into your dreams, it is time to banish obstacles, be they fears that lurk in the hidden recesses of your mind, or more tangible problems. They may seem insurmountable, the effort required to even start tackling them immense, but Kangaroo counsels that once you gather your mental and physical reserves and make that first leap forward, events will take on their own momentum and you, like Kangaroo, will have no option but to go forward as your burdens fall behind you.

Kangaroo reproduces constantly, but never allows the nourishing milk that feeds this rich output to be over consumed. Her tiny neonate suckles delicately at a nipple but the fertilized egg in her womb must remain dormant until her first-born starts to forage for grass as well as suckle – only then does the egg develop and her next child make its wondrous journey to her pouch and its rich milk supply. Kangaroo then mates again, and so the carefully synchronized cycle continues. Kangaroo counsels against spreading your own energy too widely. Time and energy are finite; squandering energy on ten projects prevents any one blossoming to fruition. That is the wisdom of Kanagaroo.

KOOKABURRA & OTHER KINGFISHERS

LIGHTENING YOUR LIFE · DIVING INTO EXPERIENCE

KOOKABURRA, quintessential Australian, denizen of aromatic eucalyptus bush and woodland alike, wakes the earth with her laughter. She is harbinger of the sun, called upon by the first Aborigine spirits to tell them when it was time to kindle the sparkling fire that would light all of Gaia for another day. If Kookaburra has chuckled in your dreams it is time to lighten your life and let inspiration, delight, even divinity, shine through. Great spiritual masters laugh with joy at the wonders of life, and Kookaburra counsels so should you.

Laughter loosens ties in our minds and like solar rays is a source of creativity and energy. When we habitually walk through life with faces set in stern disapproving expressions, our arms crossed in defensive offense, we can't help but feel those emotions. Being aware of these habitual postures and altering them can revolutionize our lives. Just dropping our arms and smiling immediately changes the way we feel. Suddenly we really are sunnier and our minds, jogged out of gloom we didn't even know we were in, start to think anew. Possibility is regained.

Kookaburra, when she retires for the night on a welcoming branch, nestles closely with her family in warmth and friendship. Most social of birds, she knows you too need to surround yourself with others. Letting laughter into your life means other people will see you differently, too. Friends will suddenly linger over a glass of wine, and strangers smile back. The future is sunlit, not cloudy.

Kookaburra, as other Kingfisher spirits do, dives expertly for her prey, be it venomous Snake, darting Lizard, or burrowing Worm. By an English stream, an incomparable flash of vivid turquoise-blue glinting off dappled water means Kingfisher has seen Minnow. She plunges through the surface, spears her snack and with beating wings regains her perch. African Pygmy Kingfisher dives through hazy green rainforest for succulent insects. None knows the meaning of hesitation. As your guide, Kookaburra tells you that the time has come to abandon stagnation, to dive into life, to embrace the multiplicity of experiences it offers. Now.

LION

Tawny monarch of the vast savannah, Lion stretches, Lion yawns and roars, Lion luxuriates under the deep azure blue of wide African skies. Lion does not waste her days in needless physical exertion, but for twenty-one hours out of twenty-four conserves her energy by sleeping, resting, and companionably lounging. Although she can easily bring down hard-muscled Zebra or meaty, horned Wildebeest, and in alliance bull giraffes weighing over a ton (1,000 kg), regal Lion sees no shame in scavenging her dinner whenever possible.

As your guide she counsels that working long hours solely to obtain prestige items exhausts both body and spirit and leaves little room for more ultimately rewarding ways of passing time, such as those offered by the pleasures of friendship. Lion meanders through her pride's expansive domain or relaxes in its shade sometimes alone, but usually with three or four others for company. The pride itself, usually numbering around forty, rarely meets all together in one place, but Lion shows her respect and delight in belonging to this larger community by acknowledging fellow members with an affectionate greeting ceremony. Soft, solicitous, mutual moaning wells from deep inside Lion and her familiar's body to be followed ritually by mutual head-rubbing and flank-leaning, while tails drape comfortingly over one another's backs. Sometimes Lion, forgetting her great strength, leans so enthusiastically in her pleasure that both sink to the ground.

Loneliness is spirit-diminishing – solitary confinement the most awful of punishments. We wither and die, sometimes inside, sometimes literally, without the support and society of others and often we don't even realize the source of our distress. If Lion has come to you, it is to remind you how vital friends and neighbors really are. The sun radiates from beneficent Lion. To bask in its life-affirming warmth, reach out and be open to others. This is the wisdom of Lion.

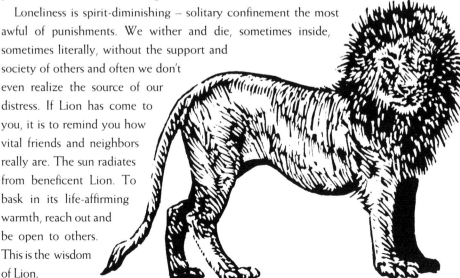

LIZARD

LETTING GO · DISTRACTING OPPONENTS

SOMETIMES GAUDY in the brilliance of her color, sometimes so cryptic she can be mistaken for a leaf, scurrying, agile Lizard is peerless. A predator of first degree, whether she is Komodo Dragon who may devour Pig in a single meal or Gecko, who dines on fat Housefly, Lizard is amazing. Female Lizard can often reproduce without the need for males, or their sperm, creating perfect tiny clones of herself. Sometimes Lizard does this when males are in short supply sometimes to vastly increase her population – after all, in a unisexual world all Lizard's offspring can generate new life. Lizard, then, is the ultimate survivor, and teaches that we can easily do without the things we once thought essential.

Her tail vertebrae contain weak links that allow her tail to break off with ease. Although it is a fifth limb, often prehensile, and used for running, swimming, climbing, balancing, in passionate courtship, and as a storehouse of nutritious fat to sustain Lizard in times of famine, she will sacrifice it if necessary. When predator threatens keenly, Lizard sways her tail from side to side taking her aggressor's attention from her plump, tasty body before shedding it. The still living limb wriggles convulsively, distracting her enemy and allowing Lizard to escape with life, if not limb. Her tail grows back not exactly as it was, but still able to do everything its owner could wish for.

If dry, warm, ingenious Lizard darts around you as you dream, or she unexpectedly crosses your path on a sunny morning, the time has come to let go. All too often we hang on to people and possessions that threaten our physical well-being, our peace of mind: the controlling partner – who will surely change – for fear of being alone; the money-draining, ulcer-inducing house, because we are anxious not to downsize lest the neighbors view us with disdain. Lizard counsels that there are times when that crucial shedding must be done. Something will soon fill the gap and it is, as Lizard and you in your heart know, a simple matter of survival.

LANGUR MONKEY

FIGHTING FOR JUSTICE · THE FRUITS OF VICTORY

Langur, sacred Indian descendent of the Hindu monkey god Hanuman, ranges from the high slopes of the Himalayas to Rajasthan's deciduous forests, and even semi-desert. She swings on a long, prehensile tail from urban balconies and temple roofs and haunts shady groves, her black face peering mischievously at a curious world while her thick creamy fur, seen against a background of streaming sunshine, lends her a sparkling halo of white light – surely a befitting beatification for one who is Hanuman-made. To rescue Sita, beloved wife of Lord Rama, who had been stolen by the King of Lanka, Hanuman journeyed the length of India to the King's island realm where he was captured and had burning bundles of wood were tied to his tail. But wily Hanuman ran wildly through the isle setting it alight before plunging into the Indian Ocean to put out his tail before finally delivering Sita. To humanity he now gives these attributes of speed, agility, and cunning with which any obstacle may be overcome.

Langur has bounded into your dreams to remind you that her ancestor's victory was that of good against evil, of the normal man prevailing against overwhelming power. He also counsels that you too fight for justice, no matter what the odds. You may have been wrongly accused of petty theft, another may have stolen your livelihood using deceit, or a corporation may be seeking to ride roughshod over your rights to an unpolluted world where others are not exploited. Langur bids you not to be downhearted. The weapons your opponents would use to best you can be turned against them to great effect. And Langur has the skills to defeat those who would seek to violate your civil liberties and those of common humanity. In the forest his piercing alarm call warns all of the approach of Tiger and Panther and you will just as surely expose those who would treat you with malfeasance. With Langur by your side as you journey, a new way of approaching injustice will reveal itself and you will surely taste the fruits of victory and the discomfort of your enemies.

LLAMA

STRENGTH IN GENTLENESS • LETTING GO OF FEAR

Nine million years ago, lovely gentle Llama walked across fertile California. Now she traverses rugged paths in the high mountains of Bolivia, Chile, and Peru, but treading so lightly, so delicately, on her two-toed feet that she damages not even the softest of soils.

Llama is sweet-tempered, soft, sociable, and friendly, but her beautiful wide-eyed face belies her ability to withstand harsh, unforgiving conditions. She can live in the rarefied atmospheres sixteen thousand feet (4,880 m) above sea level, graze on the driest of pasture, and survive days without water. Sleeping with her feet tucked beneath her body, her wondrous thick, extraordinarily tough hair hanging over her flanks, she prefers to remain in rain and snow rather than seek shelter. But even fair Llama will defend herself if provoked, spitting a thick regurgitated mass of semi-digested grass into her aggressor's face, where it sticks, greenly.

If Llama has come to your journeyings, consider your way in the world. Do you stride heavily to convince others that you are tough and rough? Do you walk with attitude, swaggering and fierce, or serenely like companionable Llama?

Your guide counsels that a harsh, defensive manner keeps other people far away while drawing near loneliness and disrespect. Llama has no need to swagger for she is truly strong within. She spits only as a last resort, for the taste in her mouth is foul and stays with her just as the unpleasant effects of unwarranted, overbearing behavior stay within us.

Often this way of being has its roots in fear. Llama has come to your side to help you let go of your angst and forebodings, perhaps by giving you the courage to consult the wisdom of another who may untangle the psychology of your mind. Llama's wisdom is hard, but there is no path so impassable that Llama cannot walk it. If you will allow her to guide and support you, you will rediscover the sweetness in your soul and the natural affability that will make you as one with others.

MALLARD DUCK

THE FOLLY OF MATERIAL GREED · FEELING AT HOME

W HEN ONE OF the Buddha's earthly human forms died, he was incarnated as glorious Golden Mallard. Without their husband, his wife and children were reduced to living on charity. He flew quickly on shimmering wing to save them from their misery and promised to give them one of his feathers of beaten gold every few weeks so that they might sell them and live in ease and comfort. Soon his wife grew greedy and trapped Golden Mallard when he came with his gift, plucking him bare. But his feathers, having been mercilessly stolen, not freely given, became white like Crane's and without material worth. In time Golden Mallard's wings grew back and he flew far, far away from his family, never to return. If iridescent-headed Mallard has flown across your path or landed at your feet, he asks that you meditate upon the meaning of material greed and its consequences for you, your children, humanity, and all of Gaia's animal spirits who now so need your protection.

On water Mallard is elegant, beautiful, and supremely at ease. He dives surely and when he surfaces water rolls in great glistening streaks from sleek plumage. He moves with consummate ease down man's canals and on deep reservoirs, across clear icy lakes and rushing rivers. With a rushing of powerful wings, he springs vertically from the water's surface and flies peerlessly through northern skies. Yet when Mallard walks on land he is a comic figure, a clown waddling from side to side on large, bright orange feet. As your guide, Mallard counsels that you seek out environments you feel at home in. He moves in the waters of emotion and the air of spirit and knowledge. If you feel ill at ease and awkward with those who surround you, be they friends, colleagues, or neighbors, particularly if their values are centered on the materialism of earth, Mallard counsels it is time to seek out those who make you feel warm and comfortable inside, who share your values and aspirations. For then, every day will be lit with happiness and fulfillment. This is the wisdom of Mallard.

MEERKAT

EQUALITY · FRATERNITY · CELEBRATING DIVERSITY

Little Meerkat, most sociable of creatures, lives in the dry, open African savannah. To protect herself from the predators and extremes of temperature this terrain brings, she lives in a complex maze of underground corridors which run on two or three levels stretching as widely as thirty yards (25 meters) square with up to ninety entrances. Meerkat does not live here alone – she shares her quarters with Ground Squirrel and Yellow Mongoose, and around thirty others of her kind. And Meerkat is the embodiment of gregarious equality, for in her colonies rank simply does not exist. And without the need for dominance, what need can there be to compete or fight? At night Meerkat curls with others in soft piles in warmth and amicability. During the day, she loves to play.

But Meerkat's easy going behavior belies her alert disposition. Long after sunrise, the first cautious Meerkat nose appears from the warren. Eyes keenly check the horizon for danger, for swooping Hawk, for vigilant Eagle. Slowly, head and shoulders follow until finally she emerges to sit upright in her sentry position. One by one Meerkat's companions gather, sunbathing to replace the warmth the cold night steals, gamboling gamely but still alert. After a while, one Meerkat or another decides it is time to seek the fat grubs, the beetle larvae she loves to munch on, drops on all fours and scurries off with the rest of the colony following.

Meerkat asks you to consider if you are being too competitive, too strident in your relationships. Are you wasting time, life, and energy fighting for position and rank when you could be enjoying company and friendship? Are you suffering from status anxiety? Over-sensitively taking offence? Being mean?

Meerkat can be a fearsome foe. She rips the sting from Scorpion and devours her mercilessly, but shares her bounty. She is keen and skillful in defense, but only when she has real reason. Meerkat counsels you that, like her, you rejoice in amity and closeness, also re-membering that you are neither better nor worse than other people in your life, simply different. And there is no reason to fight over that.

MOLE

GLOSSY VELVET-FURRED MOLE lives within the very earth itself. Her subterranean lair providing all she needs, Mole rarely, if ever, ventures to its surface. Safe from predators and the extremes of temperature that make life so difficult for many, Mole must nonetheless dig hard for her living. Unique in their design, her massive shoulders power great paddle-like paws, allowing Mole to tunnel through thirteen feet (4 m) of soil in sixty seconds and disappear below ground in five. However, having excavated her extensive networks Mole scurries constantly along her tunnels, for they are not only her home but her larder. Insects and, in particular, Worm drop like manna from heaven – for these Mole-made gaps act as extremely effective pit-traps. So plentiful is Mole's supply of food that Worm is often paralyzed with a bite and placed in storage where stocks of a thousand or more may build up. An extremely impressive way to remain plump yet svelte, Mole consumes a staggering eight thousand worms a year.

If Mole has tunneled into your life, shamanistic journeying to the non-ordinary realities of the Lower World may prove particularly rewarding, for the wisdom of its spirits can reveal answers to questions that have been troubling you for the longest of times.

If feeling below par, the soil's riches are there to replenish you: essential minerals, iron, vitamin-rich earthy foods such as carrots and celeriac, and purifiers such as garlic and ginger can all reenergize and revitalize.

Mole has chosen to guide you because she understands that being grounded and possessing the self-knowledge that allows you to present a genuine face to the world is now of paramount importance. Pretentious and false behavior, so often based on fear of failure or worry about our position in society, can only impede material and emotional progress. Mole counsels that you look within and accept yourself for what you are. Admitting our flaws and our talents alike, even to ourselves takes courage and no little effort. But as Mole soon harvests lasting plenty from the earth after grueling toil, you too will find that the treasures you have been seeking fall at your feet.

MONGOOSE

FREEDOM FROM PEOPLE PESTS • TAKING INITIATIVE

Lissome Mongoose has trotted alertly along well-worn track, through grass tussock and underground tunnel for thirty million years, her form entirely unchanged, testament to its marvelous design.

Fearless, Mongoose is "direct, open and headlong in her attack"[*] moving at a bounding gallop. Utterly agile she may ricochet off a rock to change direction and jump three feet (1 m) with practiced ease. Even Cobra, her deadly venom and lightening strike feared by all of India's mammals, dreads the whirlwind approach of Mongoose. Partially immune to Cobra's venom and easily able to avoid her bite, Mongoose seizes Cobra's lowered head after her ineffectual strike. She slices through flesh and crunches on bone. The contest is over. Cobra is vanquished.

If Mongoose has run into your dreams, raced with you as you journeyed, she has many wisdoms to convey and among these is to consult the magic of Cobra, who holds many secrets that may transform your world. Mongoose first helped Man rid his home and his granaries of Rat, Mouse and Scorpion in the ancient Chaldean city of Ur, millennia upon millennia ago. Today Mongoose counsels that you, too, rid yourself of pests, of the people who irritate you, are jealous of you and hold you back. Mongoose is fit, flexible and lithe – a disciplined, fierce, furred guerrilla. She counsels that the physical fitness that endows you with dynamic activity will find you victorious in the mental fights of life, the cut-throat jostling for position. Mind and body are one, meaning a body that can react with speed and energy has its counterpart in a razor-sharp mind. Mongoose counsels that there is no better way to achieve this edge than to practice the transforming warrior disciplines, the martial arts of Kung Fu, of Tai Chi.

The time has come to take the initiative, to dissemble no more, push false modesty aside and openly, with utter confidence, run for the position you crave. As Cobra succumbs to the power of Mongoose so opposition to you, no matter how highly placed, will fall.

[*] *The Book of Indian Animals*, S H Prater

MOOSE

Mʏᴛʜɪᴄ ᴍᴏᴏsᴇ, primal in her power, still ranges mysteriously through the world's great northern forests, and swims underwater seeking green salty nourishment. Broad hooves support her on saturated boggy ground, strong legs propel her through rapid rivers to find sanctuary on islands when nurturing her calves. Water is her element as much as land – Penobscot Indians believe that she evolved from the whale, and zoologists believe that she and Whale originate from the same prehistoric stock, aligning her with ancient earth-mother power and the feminine energies of intuition and illumination.

As your guide, she reminds you to emotionally nurture both those around you and yourself, so that your life and projects may flourish. She asks you to look within and shows you how to move from the material world to inner meditation, which will bring clarity, allowing you to discern new approaches and revealing which path to take in times of crucial decision. If something feels wrong, trust your intuition, for your guide's senses are acute. Appearances are deceptive; Moose relies not on vision but on smell and hearing. She favors the crepuscular hours when the barriers between worlds rarefy, so journey to seek her guidance as the sun's brilliance becomes dimmed in the heavens, then contemplate the challenges of life.

Moose weighs eighteen hundred pounds (815 kg) yet moves surely, silently, and quickly through her woody domain. Confident and strong, Moose does not seek safety within a herd; she takes her own decisions and vigorously defends herself and her calf with mighty charges and powerful kicks from sharp hooves. She teaches that self-reliance develops character and the ability to overcome adversity.

Male moose advertises his presence and sexuality by urine marking and by thrashing vegetation with his massive antlers, but for all his power Moose is patient. If a female is ready for his attentions he mates dynamically; if not, he waits patiently with her until she finally becomes receptive. Rushing into love is to court failure. Let love come in its own time, creating a relationship of trust, profundity, and true meaning.

MOUNTAIN GOAT

DEFENDING LOVE • UNDERSTANDING VULNERABILITY

HIGH IN THE MISTY cold mountains, dainty Goat leaps sure-footedly from crag to crag, far away from earth-bound predators. Her only foe is sharp-eyed Golden Eagle, capable of knocking her from her rocky promontory or seizing a kid. Those whom Goat has chosen to guide should study the ways of mighty Eagle, pre-eminent predator of the northern skies, to understand where their own vulnerabilities lie.

Goat is supremely adapted to this unforgiving terrain. She descends steep rock chutes in virtual free fall, breaking her speed by bouncing from wall to wall while her hooves, with stiff outer rims and flexible pads, not only absorb landing shock but provide leaping spring. She counsels that you, too, spend time perfecting your own arts, be they burnishing hearth and home, or diving beneath the rolling sea, so that you may brook indecision and be sure of your dealings in your own world.

Goat moves with confidence along the narrowest of ledges and, if you seek her in your journeying, will guide you to your path through life – no matter how faint it at first appears. Wild goats of Sind carry within their belly *bezoar*, a hard secretion regarded through out Europe and the East as an antidote to poison and remedy for disease. Wise, mystical, sagacious Goat, inhabiting the land among the clouds, so near to other worlds, reminds you that the remedies for life's problems lie within yourself. Journey, and they will be revealed.

Goat also possesses intense sexual energy. The male American mountain goat reeks constantly of musk to advertise his masculine qualities to the world at large, and his mountain-top harem in particular. He fights fiercely for his sexual rights, dispatching rivals with sharp horns. If he fails in its defense, his harem surely will be taken by another.

Goat counsels that you too must fight for love, not with violence but with word and deed. Defend your own love with thoughtfulness and with passion, celebrate it with the gift of wild rose or the full moon seen on a wild night, and love will remain yours forever.

MOUSE

PERSISTENCE • THE PROTECTION OF SCRUTINY

TINIEST, MOST FRAGILE and delicate of creatures, Harvest Mouse weighs less than half an ounce (14 g) yet thrives and belongs to the greatest and most successful family of mammals on earth. Light and nimble, Harvest Mouse climbs mighty swaying golden corn stalks to harvest their grain. Laid next to her diminutive head, just one seed stretches from eye to nose tip. Surely its tough woody covering would be impenetrable to one so diminutive, so dainty?

But behind her gentle, shining eyes and tremulous whiskers lies the secret of Mouse's success – her incredible self-sharpening teeth. Two front teeth, top and bottom, consist of an exceptionally hard front layer of enamel backed by dentine. As Mouse gnaws, the dentine wears away and the enamel is honed to an edge so sharp that she and her cousins can, eventually, break through any shell no matter how hard, how dense, to the soft delicious center within. For Mouse, no obstacle is so tough that it cannot be overcome.

As your guide, she counsels the wisdom of persistence and reminds you of the strength of the seemingly unassuming. You too can achieve your goal, be it finally getting a publishing deal or moving into another plane in meditation if, like Mouse, you really want to. Many predators would like to dine on Mouse, plump from the energy-rich vital seeds she consumes – Cat stalks her in the long grass, Fox pounces swiftly, Eagle seeks to grasp Mouse in her sharp talons. A rustle in the corn, the fall of a shadow, an infinitesimal tremor transmitted through the earth are of the greatest of import for Mouse. All may be harbingers of death, and none may necessarily be what they seem. Mouse advises that you scrutinize everything and give no one your trust until they have earned it: Does that mega-expensive lawyer have your best interests at heart, or his? Like Mouse, look beyond the obvious to the pattern within and see the seemingly trivial for what it is – a part of a larger whole. Thus may you chart a safe path through an ever more complex and unstable world.

OCTOPUS

TAKING THE FUTURE INTO YOUR OWN HANDS

Octopus lurks in her undersea lair waiting patiently for her favorite morsel, succulent Crab, to sidle unwarily by. A tentacle-like arm lies discretely coiled, its latent power yet to be revealed. It unwinds slowly and stealthily but strikes ruthlessly, suckers making vice-like contact. Octopus draws Crab into her chamber and devours her at leisure.

Octopus also hunts Crab in the open sea – arms rise above her, outstretched like a floating parachute, before descending and enveloping Crab in a cloud of flesh. She even leaves her green salty empire, exchanging sustaining water for earth's air, as she slithers over damp rocks to where Crab innocently basks. Octopus does not wait for fate to deliver Crab; she employs whatever strategy is necessary to capture her delight.

Octopus has swum into your journeyings to bid you to follow the desires of your heart wherever they may take you. If your partner has left for a faraway land, join them; if a new exciting possibility calls from distant climes, embrace it as firmly as Octopus does Crab. If your heart yearns for art school while your body commutes to the city, raise a loan, fly in the face of what others might deem sensible, and in a new city become a student once more.

Octopus covers her skin with pigment cells on a magical, iridescent background. When she contracts or expands these cells her body changes color, revealing intense emotions. When annoyed by external events she turns herself rosy red; when frightened, disturbed, or unsure, the side of her body facing the irritant signals her displeasure by paling. When decidedly furious, her body shrieks its message in livid white. But Octopus knows caution also, and if she deems her foe insurmountable she cloaks her retreat in a veil of ink. Octopus counsels that you, too, show your emotions. If you pretend disinterest when your dream comes calling, do not be surprised if it melts silently away. If others obstruct you, let them know your anger so that they may desist – if they continue, like wise Octopus keep your movements secret until the future is incontrovertibly yours.

OPOSSUM

VICTORY THROUGH STRATEGY · RISING ABOVE MALICE

OVER THE MILLENNIA, much-whiskered Opossum has slowly extended her range northward through the Americas, from the balmy south to icy-wintered Canada. She seems unstoppable but her naked tail, with which she hangs upside down from branches to feast on fruit and nuts, and acts as a fifth limb, is particularly vulnerable to the ravages of frostbite.

But Opossum's long evolution in South America comes with an enormous advantage. She is immune to the venom of Snake: her blood pressure and heartbeat remain steady, and she suffers no allergic reaction or terrible hemorrhaging. Opossum dines on meaty Copperhead and Rattlesnake when other seemingly more viable opponents of Snake must flee.

If Opossum has chosen to swing into your journeyings, consider how you react to the venom and spitefulness of others. Unlike her, does your heart beat violently in your chest with anger, does your blood pressure rise just as it would if you had been bitten by Snake? Opossum counsels calm, for you are damaging only yourself. Let their words and deeds wash through and over you. Then, with a clear mind and objective plan, you may decisively counter their malice.

When threatened by a foe mightier than herself Opossum feigns death, making herself a very unattractive prospect by drooling saliva, emitting a vile stench from her anal glands, and often defecating to add a final smelly touch to the convincing picture. Sometimes when events are overwhelming, like Opossum it is advantageous to put on a supreme act. By showing vulnerability and fear we can open ourselves up to further onslaughts. By passively standing our ground, no matter how much we may be trembling inside, we still have a chance to survive, even to come out on top. And if all else fails, like Opossum, we, too, can drop our act and attack fiercely – if overly prodded in her death-like state she suddenly becomes very much alive, snarling and gnashing fifty hard, white teeth. Our foe is surprised, unnerved, off balance. In a flash of opportunity, we may strike and win. Victory by strategy tastes sweet, and will prove long-lasting.

ORANG-UTAN

TAKING THE TIME TO LIVE • SIMPLE PLEASURES

ORANG-UTAN'S COMPLEX cultures and traditions stretch back over fourteen million years, during which time he has lived in utter contentment and in peaceful harmony with the arboreal world which sustains him so munificently.

As dusk falls Orang-utan, by bending branches high in the trees, weaves a safe platform that he cushions with thick, soft leaves. Twigs which might irritate and disturb his slumbers are assiduously removed, and if rain seems likely he fashions a roof before retiring beneath distant twinkling stars and the warm rain forest canopy. Orang-utan appreciates his creature comforts. When dawn breaks, Orang-utan sees no need to leap from bed, if tired he snoozes peacefully till noon, and always greets his day gently with measured thought. Breathing deeply, he removes stale air from his tremendous lungs, rubs russet brown eyes, and stretches his body and great long limbs. After breakfasting unhurriedly on delicious ripe durian or fragrant honey dextrously procured from combs deep in the protective crannies of trees, he returns to his bed to sleep in the gentle rays of the sun before carrying on with the business of his day.

Orang-utan understands the true value of time, and counsels that you, too, use it wisely. Modern urban society places great value on speed and rush. To be deprived of sleep and to sacrifice a leisurely lunch to work longer, harder, and ultimately less efficiently for another, is lauded. Orang-utan has swung into your dreams that you may consider if you are working in order to live, or living merely to work. Does your heart race with anxiety as you run for the subway? Do you wake exhausted? Is your job taking so much of your time and energy that you are missing out on those very experiences which make us human – the sharing of food and laughter with friends, walking in the countryside and hearing the music of the birds, or seeing a rainbow sparkle at the end of the world? If so, Orang-utan counsels that you adjust your priorities lest time slip silently away, taking pleasure and love with it.

OSTRICH

FACING REALITY · UNDERSTANDING WHAT IS POSSIBLE

ONCE OSTRICH FLEW. Then, sixty-five million years ago, a vast body from outer space collided with earth. The power of this monumental explosion created debris so great, so dense, that it blocked out the sun for weeks, perhaps months. The gigantic reptiles who ruled sky and earth perished but Bird survived, and when the sun again bathed the earth she colonized not only the skies but its now empty predator-free landscape.

Ostrich still retains the light fantastic knowledge of air but is solid and grounded by choice. His vast three-hundred-and-thirty pound (150 kg) body pounds across the African savanna at forty-four miles per hour (70 km/h), his mate's eggs are hatched in its warm, welcoming soil and he swallows stones and glittering diamonds to break down the copious plant material in his forty-six feet (14-m) intestine.

If Ostrich has thundered into your journeying, consider how grounded you are. Is your mind always drifting on impractical flights of fancy? Do your credit card bills remain unopened while your debt soars? Does your mind whirl and eddy? Living in the city means that we no longer have contact with soil. The energy from our bodies is dispersed over hard concrete, rather than earthing us.

Ostrich counsels that walking on open land, through wood and field, can calm your mind and let your energy settle. For Ostrich knows it is time to be practical lest reality slip away. One day there maybe no more credit and instead of having honed our fancies into material form, we find they have been scattered on the four winds. Sometimes it is difficult to face this reality, because we feel if we lose our dreams we lose a part of our soul. But Ostrich is still in touch with the wonders of air. His fabulous wing plumes may be soft, unfit for flight, but their black-and-white beauty is undimmed while within he carries the diamond's hard knowledge. You may not be able to make your castles in the air take on substance, but with Ostrich by your side the practical can also be the fabulous.

OTTER

FLEXIBILITY · LATERAL THINKING

Otter, graceful, lithe athlete, frolics joyously in her watery domain. One of its most intelligent and ingenious hunters, Otter is always discovering new ways to catch her dinner. She will puncture Beaver's consummately constructed dam, wait for the water level to drop, and then feast on the fat, trapped fish. When lakes are covered with ice she will hunt bluegill and "consume them at leisure"*; she digs in mud for crayfish, pulls unwary floating ducks to their doom, and darts after fish. Sea Otter, floating lazily on her back, puts the stone on her stomach and uses it as an anvil to fracture Crab whom she has seized in the salty depths.

If Otter has swum into your journeyings it is to remind you that there are many ways of approaching a problem. Too often we suffer from tunnel vision, thinking there is only one way to make money or even bake a chocolate cake. There are hundreds of recipes for chocolate cake – if you lack icing sugar for a fondant topping and the store is shut, it doesn't mean that you can't make a cake, merely that you must make a different one, which will also be delicious. Otter counsels that you think laterally. If your life has been carrying on in one deep-worn groove, it is time to skip a track.

Otter works hard for her living. Sea Otter must consume one-third of her body weight every day, but she never ceases to play with glee. She slides down grassy banks as happily as a child sledding in the snow; drops pebbles into the water and dives after them, intent on catching them before they hit the bottom; balances stones on her head like a circus performer, and plays tag and wrestles with others. Otter delights in every moment of her day. Otter is never bored. Like Otter, work and play hard and you, too, will exult in your days.

* *Mammals of North America*, Adrian Forsyth

SEEKING THE HIDDEN · WHITE MAGIC

Owl GLIDES SILENTLY through ancient brooding forests, their trees laden with snow glittering in the light of a pale, cold moon. All seems still as Owl lands high in the branches of a towering pine to survey her wild lands. For mortals a hush has descended on the world, but for Owl the forest is alive with sound. Beneath the carpet of snow Mouse nibbles warily on a still green leaf, Mole scurries through her underground realm, and far in the distance Wolf's footfall crunches on fragile ice.

Owl's ears are not symmetrical, one being higher than the other, and sound is channeled separately into each ear by a ruff of fine feathers. Owl hears in perfect stereo, allowing her to pinpoint the trembling rodent far below. She swoops noiselessly, giving Mouse no intimation of her fate, hovers to focus on the sound of Mouse's tiny bites – then pounces and takes her to her aerie, clutched in razor-sharp talons. Owl swallows her warm, furry meal whole.

The next day Owl rests – a feathered statue – but inside her powerful gizzard grinds Mouse, separating nourishing meat from bone and fur, which she regurgitates as a neat, compact ball.

If Owl on strong majestic wings has flown into your world, she knows that the time has come for you to seek that which is hidden. Arcane knowledge deep within the ageless traditions of white magic will now reveal itself if you quiet your mind and take the time to explore the mysteries beyond with a guide or those who have the same mystical goals. Like Owl, you will absorb the benign and nourishing, and discard that which is destructive. The web connecting the world and the universe to planes we cannot even see will become clear, and imbue your life with intense meaning.

On a material level, Owl counsels that you look far beyond the surface actions of others. If you trust to your own intuitions and perceptions, others will be unable to deceive you – their hidden agendas will be as clear as a flower in sunlight, and Owl's wisdom will be yours.

PANDA

TRANQUILITY · SELF-SUFFICIENCY

GENTLE, TRANQUIL PANDA sleeps blissfully in her bamboo grove, her fat, succulent body slumping against a thick log, snow providing a soft cushion, her profuse deep fur keeping bitter cold at bay. Self-contained and content, she seeks no company in her serried banks of bamboo, so dense that the light which penetrates from the wide sky above takes on a soft greenish hue. Panda stares intensely at those who would intrude on her world of plenty and ease – her great black eye patches making the message that she wants nothing but to be left alone, tangible and unmistakable. Legend says that having discovered that a Chinese girl had died saving her from Leopard, Panda in gratitude held a funeral. Weeping copiously she rubbed her eyes on her black armband of mourning and the dye stained her face fur forever – but only Panda knows the truth.

If Panda has come to your dreams she knows that the time has come for you, too, to find inner contentment and to understand the value of self-sufficiency. Sometimes our worlds become too wrapped up in other people's – we become dependent upon their approval and wither inside if they withhold it. Panda counsels that visiting retreats will fortify your soul, allowing your true self, not someone else's image of you, to flourish. Happiness does not rest on interdependence but on the inner strength that allows true independence of spirit, which in its turn gives rise to fruitful relationships based on mutual respect. This can be a hard path to follow, but if you let her, compassionate Panda will walk with you until you can walk alone.

Panda is a specialist, placidly dining on the shoots of bamboo, fluidly tearing their woody sheaths in order to reach the more succulent growth within. However, in salutation to her carnivorous past, Panda still eats fragrant flesh provided by others. She counsels that you, too, look back to your roots, your earlier life lessons, and digest the wisdom that these past experiences have bequeathed you. When you can achieve this, you may better deal with what the future will now bring.

SUNSHINE AND LIGHT THERAPY · ANIMAL LANGUAGE

Scarlet, hyacinth, azure, violet, yellow, Parrot is wondrous and vivid, Parrot's plumage is of the rainbow, her demeanor that of the sun. Color and light affect us in so many different ways – gray cloud depresses us, red surroundings stimulate our appetites – and each color has its own wavelength and energy that is absorbed by our eyes, our skin, our electromagnetic aura, influencing our physical, emotional, and spiritual well-being. If Parrot has chosen to fly into your journeyings and dreams, color therapy will help you balance your life – yellow walls can lead to a more optimistic way of seeing life, blue have a calming affect. Environment is now everything.

If you live in a land where winter is long, the days are short, and sunshine is rare, changes to your biochemistry can leave you depressed and fatigued. Parrot counsels visiting lands of sunshine which will stimulate your energy and revitalize your soul. If your heart has been telling you to move but your mind has been finding reasons not to, Parrot has come to tell you to follow your intuition.

Parrot does not possess a larynx as we do, but a syrinx at the bottom of her windpipe that is divided into two tubes leading to her lungs. The mouth to each tube has fleshy lips which, like our own mouths, can open to differing degrees and in a variety of shapes – the air forced through the tube produces myriad tones and pitches. As each tube operates independently, the combination of their sounds is so immense that Parrot is able to speak to us in our own language. Ambassador supreme, the ultimate interface between human and non-human, she reminds you of the importance of listening to the language of avian music and song, and of communicating not only with fellow humans, but all the other living denizens of the earth. Words you hear in the fluting trill of birdsong will now have a particular significance for you, and if Parrot chooses to speak to you in your own language as you journey, mark her words well. Their import may change your life.

PEACOCK

HARMONY IN DIVERSITY · PROTECTION

THE CALL OF PEACOCK is loud and raucous, echoing wildly to warn all the inhabitants of forest and jungle that the mighty predator Tiger is patrolling and stalking her territories. Peacock is also a killer of snakes and may even be seen with hooded Cobra grasped in her claws.

As your guide, Peacock embodies the need for protection. She counsels you to be alert to the intentions of those around you. It is no jungle secret that Cobra and Tiger can be dangerous, and so it is in the world of man. The double-dealer and the heartbreaker are known. Peacock advises that you avoid them and that you also take time to understand the wisdom of Tiger and Cobra and their connection to her.

Peacock is the most exquisite of birds. Cosmic vehicle of Kama, Hindu god of love, male Peacocks' feathers shimmer with gold, green, and blue iridescence, hundreds of eyes flashing as he displays this wonder, dancing before the hen he wishes to take as his mate.

Yet Peacock, for all her glory, flamboyance, and noise is modest and sensitive. If disturbed she slides quietly into the jungle, and rarely has been seen consummating her love, leading to a folkloric belief that Peahen fertilizes her eggs with a glittering jewel presented to her by her consort.

Peacock's tail drops after courtship and she counsels that although the first declarations of love may be attended by the flourishing of rainbow flowers or offerings of ambrosial foods in luxurious surroundings, true intimacy develops after this, in seclusion and simplicity. Outward show is a ritual, but it is not the reality of a long-lasting relationship.

Wheel-like in structure, male Peacock's tail is symbolic of the eternal cycles of life, while its "eyes" represent the all-seeing munificent, life-giving sun. Peacock reminds those she has chosen to guide that the harmony inherent in the splendid diversity of her form is reflected on earth. Celebrate life's multiplicity, and by doing so gain inner tranquility and the fertile seeds of creativity.

PENGUIN

PATIENCE NURTURES RADICAL CHANGE

Penguin once flew through blue Antarctic skies and skimmed over southern oceans, diving elegantly and swimming beneath the waters to feast on fish. As hundreds of thousands of years went by, Penguin swam more and flew less. Finally her wings became flippers, she exchanged the light hollow bones of flight for those that were dense and solid allowing her to remain beneath the water's surface with ease, and her feathers, now anointed with oil to prevent water penetrating her skin and leaching her warmth, became short and stiff with a downy undercoat. Penguin left the wonder of flight and the freedom of the skies behind her in exchange for an incomparable mastery of the seas.

As your guide, Penguin counsels that change, no matter how radical, is always possible if you are prepared to be patient. We cannot become new people overnight, but if we are prepared to accept that change takes time, and believe in our hearts that the cumulative effect of hundreds of tiny changes are in the end monumental, we can in the end do anything. Penguin knows that inside a three-hundred-and-fifty-pound (155-kg) person heading for a heart attack is a svelte, fit beauty, although the metamorphosis will take years. Penguin counsels that you believe in yourself and take that first step into a new state of consciousness as she does when she propels her sleek black-and-white body vertically from water to land to begin the plodding hundred-mile (160-km) journey on sturdy webbed feet across unforgiving ice to reunite with chick and mate. Penguin has no doubt that she will get there, and with her guidance, so will you.

Penguin's ability to leap from water to land, from the medium of dreams to earthly mundanity, also symbolizes changes of consciousness of a different order – the waking dream. If Penguin has chosen to guide you, pay particular attention to the content of your daydreams, for they reveal your true hopes and fears, and are the catalyst to the step that could literally change your life forever.

PLATYPUS

THE INFINITE POSSIBILITIES OF CREATIVITY

P LATYPUS, MOST PHENOMENAL of mammal spirits, comprises a bill and webbed feet, sleek dense fur, and four strong limbs. Is she really the offspring of innocent Duck seduced by worldly Rat, as Aborigine tradition tells? Platypus alone knows, although if you journey to meet her in the Lower World who can say what secrets she may reveal or what mysteries she may hint at.

Certainly she combines the qualities of earth and water, of mammal and bird. Platypus can swim and dive closing her ears and eyes relying on the exquisite electrical senses of her bill to navigate and locate her food. Her young, like Duck's, first emerge in eggs, which Platypus keeps warm, nestled between her huge fat tail and her warm stomach. Yet when they hatch, like Rat's offspring, they drink milk. But Platyput, baby Platypus's, bill means she cannot suckle at a nipple and so the milk is secreted onto her mother's front, where she may scoop it up with her sensitive bill.

If Platypus has swum sleekly into your dreams, consult also the wisdom of her intimates Duck and Rat, who have much to impart. Platypus herself comes to tell you that there is no design, no conception so fantastic that it cannot be given creative form. In a world where uniformity and conformity is applauded, where mainstream entertainment is repetitive reality shows, originality is discouraged. If it hasn't been done before, those who commission or provide finance are reluctant to take the risk.

Platypus, ancient inhabitant of the ancient super-continent Gondwana, is still a success story today. She counsels that you believe in yourself, for the water she swims in is a pool of creativity – the earth she lives on is substance made real. She knows you will succeed if you base your dream firmly within the practical reality. If you have an innovative product idea, discover how it can be made, the costs involved, and how you can present it to others. Only then may you step into the world arena and court the success you will truly deserve.

POLAR BEAR

THE BENEFITS OF SPECIALIZATION

POLAR BEAR, sovereign of the high Arctic, last wilderness on earth, the ice bear, is a true specialist. His coat, thick and creamy, contains hollow hairs as well as normal fur, which act as tiny solar panels. So efficient is his insulation system that when summer comes Polar Bear makes a den deep in the permafrost to keep cool.

Wonderfully camouflaged, only Polar Bear's black nose betrays him in the roaring ice and snow, and when stalking Seal, his principal feast, he will cover it with a massive paw.

As your guide he reminds you to pay attention to detail, never sacrificing it to speed. Polar Bear knows the most skilful of hunts can be ruined by one tiny error, and so it is with any plans you are now putting into motion. Polar Bear has long legs and neck which allow him to rear up in deep snow, scan his empire visually, and catch the perfume of prey drifting on the breeze. He can smell Seal's breathing hole from three miles (5 km) away, even if it has become covered with several feet of snow. Having located the hole, Polar Bear waits patiently for Seal to surface, then his wide-reaching paw delivers a fatal blow. Sometimes, Seal's breathing hole has iced over and Polar Bear must dig down with his great curving claws with which he hauls Seal onto the ice. Seal may become suspicious as much more light than usual now penetrates his watery domain, but Polar Bear casts a shadow with his long head, fooling Seal, and dines well. So intimately connected with Seal is Polar Bear that those whom he has chosen to guide will benefit from consulting Seal's wisdom too.

Polar Bear knows every habit, every nuance, and every character trait of Seal and counsels that you, too, become a specialist. We all have unique talents but so often contemporary society demands we become generalists to survive. Polar Bear counsels that you make a supreme effort to develop your skill, be it carving wood or writing poetry, and be rewarded with the preeminence that only dedication to one field can bring.

PORCUPINE

SHARING WITH OTHERS · HIGHER KNOWLEDGE

Porcupine evolved many millions of years ago. Unchanged, he still bumbles clumsily and innocently through American forests, the long grass of the Indian Terai, and over the rocky mountains of the Himalayas. Individual, but not territorial, Porcupines often graze side by side in verdant pasture or devour the buds and leaves of winter trees in amicable silence. They share their dens – their laboriously constructed burrows, or prebuilt hollow trees – year after year, and in winter rarely potter more than a few hundred yards from home.

Porcupine teaches that the earth is bountiful and that if we share its wonders there is enough for all. Porcupine does not yearn for her neighbors' food or to live in splendid isolation in her own den, and counsels that we do not accumulate needless material possessions at the expense of others.

Porcupine lives on earth but is supremely adapted for life in the trees. Her stiff belly hairs firmly grip on rough bark while the pads and claws of her back feet act as clamps as she determinedly moves up the mightiest of trunks. A tree is a traditional shamanic motif connecting heaven above with the mundane world below. Listen to Porcupine carefully and she will guide you to new heights of awareness.

Porcupine trusts in the world; a creature of defense not offence, she is childlike in her innocence. But when trust is broken she defends herself fiercely by charging backward at great speed and burying the now erect and easily detached barbed quills of her back into the soft flesh of her foe. Unwitting aggressors may even impale themselves. Painful, impossible to extract and frequently deadly, almost every denizen of the natural world defers to Porcupine's power, even Tiger.

As your guide, Porcupine reminds you that the simple things in life, from a walk in the woods to a drink with old friends, give the greatest pleasure and reminds you not to become immersed in the rat race to your own detriment. Instead, live on your own terms in harmony with nature and man, garnering the respect Porcupine commands and the happiness you deserve.

PRAYING MANTIS

MEDITATION REVEALS A WAY FORWARD

PRAYING MANTIS is revered by African Bushmen as the creator of the universe, of humankind. Her inverted triangular head, with large eyes on either corner, is a dream of alien space-encounter come to earth. Did she come from ancient skies and make us flesh? Journey to the shamanic worlds of non-ordinary reality, and just maybe Mantis will tell you.

Credited with the power of prophecy on earth, she can reveal secrets unknown to guide you through life. Resting and waiting in prayer-like attitude herself, Mantis counsels that the inner silence that meditation brings will also reveal the forming pattern of your future.

Some of Mantis's kind resemble so closely deep exotic pink-red flowers that unwary Humming Bird comes to sip their nectar – and so it is important that those whom Praying Mantis has visited should also study Humming Bird's wisdom and make it their own. In an instant Mantis grasps Humming Bird in her long, serrated front legs and devours her alive, delivering a fatal bite to her neck.

But Mantis, too, can be deceived. Plump red-and-black Milkweed Bug appears to be a desirable meal, but just one taste reveals her to be toxic and disgusting. Mantis hurls her away and regurgitates copious amounts of orange fluid, removing every vestige of this impostor from her system – and never tries to eat her again. As your guide, Mantis counsels that beauty and style are deceiving and are no indication of character. The innocent-looking girl-next-door with her sweet Alice band may be a voracious gold-digger planning to divorce you with speed; the hard-looking teenager with tattoos could be the one who rescues you when you are mugged; the silicon-enhanced blonde a philosopher who also likes a good time. Look very carefully at the behavior, not the appearance, of those around you before making crucial decisions and, if you find someone poisoning your life, like Mantis, cast them and everything that might remind you of them far, far away. Beauty and ugliness really are only skin deep. And that is the wisdom of Mantis.

PYTHON

SUPPLENESS OF BODY GIVES MENTAL FLEXIBILITY

PYTHON, ANCIENT SUBLIME REPTILE, retains a vestigial bony spur on her pelvic girdle, memorial to a time when like her ancestor Lizard she, too, had four legs and walked over rock and sand, leaf litter and grass, in search of prey. Now Python has modified her body. Legion loosely articulated vertebrae, able to rotate on their neighbors, let Python coil and move her body in any direction in three-dimensional space. Python also has flexible skull bones allowing her mouth to open wide enough to devour creatures many times the diameter of her head, such as Gazelle and Deer. Extraordinarily in her suppleness, as your guide Python counsels that you too make sure that your own body can stretch and bend to its fullest ability. If we feel stiff we hold our bodies in fixed ways, our muscles become congested and go into spasm, causing us pain. And this physical rigidity translates itself into a lack of mental flexibility that makes us hold onto crystallized opinions and attitudes that no longer have relevance in our world. Watching Python and shape-shifting and dancing her magnificent, cryptic-colored form will help make your body elastic and your mind subtle and open to the new. Practicing the art of yoga will also endow you with undreamed of freedom of motion as well as a different way of seeing the world.

Python kills her living food by wrapping herself tightly around its body, preventing it from breathing and cutting off its circulation. She also coils closely around her grapefruit-sized white eggs, both camouflaging them and keeping them at a constant eighty-five degrees Farenheit (30° C). Should external temperatures drop, she raises her own by vigorously contracting her body muscles. Python stays with her babies for ninety days until, fully formed, they burst forth and slither away over the forest floor. Python holds tightly to what she needs and what she loves.

As your guide, she counsels that you pay proper attention to business associates and bosses as well as making sure of the affections of your friends and family. If others are taken for granted, closeness is lost, and soon they may leave.

RABBIT

ENJOYING THE RICHES OF LIFE

Rabbit is a soft-furred, gentle spirit. She hops happily in meadows rich with the yellow and blue flowers of springtime, and feasts on their fresh young leaves and lush grass. As she sleeps, Rabbit slowly digests her wholesome provision before excreting black ovals which still contain much rich nourishment. Canny Rabbit re-digests this food – thus extracting from it the maximum energy she can.

If Rabbit has jumped into your dreams, she has come to ask what you are absorbing from the bounty life offers. So many of us live in a major city yet never bother to spend time visiting all its museums and galleries, or enjoying its concerts and plays. We stay home alone because we can't be bothered to go out. When friends or partners come to visit we switch on the television instead of talking with them, sharing in the highs and lows of their lives and deepening our bonds. And yet we complain that we are often bored and tired. If Rabbit has come to you, she counsels that it is time to engage with life, to socialize, to feel the culture that surrounds you, and to experience a new energy and vibrancy that once you possessed but have forgotten.

Legend has it that when the Buddha summoned the creatures of the earth to bid him farewell, only twelve attended. To commemorate their devotion, he named a lunar year after each of them, in the order in which they had arrived. Fourth was wise Rabbit, who recognized the Buddha's spiritual importance. Rabbit also rules the hours of five until seven am – the time of dawn – and takes her essence from the Moon, herald of dusk and magic. During these crepuscular hours the barriers between this world and the realms of mystery, Faerie beings, ghosts, and ancestors thin, and we may gain knowledge of the future and the past and be transported to other places in time and space.

Wake at dawn when the dew bathes the grass and take a walk into Rabbit's world. Sit quietly in its magical splendor. Let your mind relax and open up to infinite possibility, and allow those who have messages for you to appear. Their revelations may astound you.

RACCOON

THROWING AWAY YOUR MASK

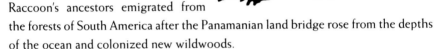

RACCOON, NATIVE TO North America, is so visible in both cities and suburbia, her inquisitive masked face peeking out from a tree hollow or behind a fire hydrant. But Raccoon's ancestors emigrated from the forests of South America after the Panamanian land bridge rose from the depths of the ocean and colonized new wildwoods.

Long white whiskers and shiny black nose serve to emphasize her mystical ebony domino. Shamans use animal masks to become other than themselves just as masqued balls liberate us by allowing us to behave as we wish without the censure of society. As your guide, Raccoon counsels that you look within to the essential you. Do you yearn to become an actor, to sell your possessions and take to the road, or practice Wicca magic? Is the face you present to the world a disguise behind which another "you" dreams and longs to be? Sometimes we hide our true selves for fear that the corporation we work for will consider us unconventional and fire us, or that our partner will call us mad.

Raccoon counsels that the process of transformation can be set in motion behind a mask, but this must be thrown away before you can finally give your essence form and truly be set free.

In Algonkian *arathcone*, the language of Algonkian Native Americans, raccoon means "he scratches with his hands", and none is more dexterous than Raccoon. When she moved to town, abandoning her traditional waterside residences, she no longer needed to open crayfish and oyster or raid Water Bird's nest, so turned her skills instead to the doors, garbage cans and lids behind which delicious delicacies lie cached, and passed on the knack of new and complex manipulations to her quick-witted offspring.

Those whom Raccoon has chosen may find it especially rewarding to make things with their hands and to learn traditional skills from another. In a world where everything can be bought from country loaves to hand-made cards, we forget that we, too, can still create beauty, be it an intricately iced cake or a terracotta bowl made on a potter's wheel.

RAT

PLENTY AND ABUNDANCE · SHREWD INTELLIGENCE

WHEN BUDDHA SUMMONED the world's animals to his side, of the twelve who came to this Supreme Master the first was perspicacious Rat. To honor these creatures Buddha gave each of their names to a twelve-year cycle and that of Rat is known to be a year of plenty. Beloved Hindu deity Shri Ganesh, who removes obstacles and blesses with success, is always accompanied by his vehicle, Rat.

Rat, sleek, shiny, and fat; judicious and intelligent, opportunist omnivore, has colonized the world. And the secret of her success? Adaptability combined with shrewd intelligence and a shining, sharp brown eye on the future. So prosperous is Indian Mole Rat, so bursting with grain that in an unusual reversal, hungry humans break into her underground stores, digging into them to steal her stock.

But Rat doesn't limit herself to grain and nuts, to roots and vegetation. In a world so populated by humanity, pickings are rich for those who care to take them: ton upon ton of abandoned pizza and hamburger, plastic, beeswax, soap. There is little that Rat spurns. But Rat is canny and approaches new substances with care. Long experience tells her an unfamiliar smell or taste may be the result of poison. Sometimes she will venture a nibble and fall ill, but she will not die, and assiduously avoid it in future. Indeed, simply smelling an unfamiliar foodstuff on the breath of an ill comrade is sufficient warning for Rat. If a choice food item is too large for one, Rat calls on eager colleagues to help move it to safety.

Rat co-operates. Rat thrives. Rat does what is necessary. Her desire to succeed is unrivalled, her success unparalleled. If vibrant Rat has chosen to guide you, you are fortunate indeed. She counsels you to be shrewd in your dealings and treat the unknown with suspicion until it is proven to be something to your advantage; that you pursue your objectives with passion, with pugnacity, with determination. And know that if you do, a time of expansion, of real plenty and abundance, is yours for the taking.

RAVEN

ARCANE KNOWLEDGE · TELEPATHIC ENERGY

Black, glossy magician of the feathered world, intelligent denizen of windswept hills, lonely crags and dark forest, Raven swoops on wings spanning four feet (1.2 m), girdling the earth. In Nordic legend he served mighty Odin as Hugin and Munin, or Thought and Memory, two Ravens who acted as the the god's eyes and ears from which the world could keep no secrets. Some say that if Raven were to leave London's great fortress – its Tower – the fall of the kingdom must follow, for Raven knows what mere mortals do not. To the augers of the City of Rome he whispered secrets of the future, and he has always called to his companion, Wolf, to tell her when a feast of Deer or Elk awaits in the woods.

If Raven's mighty *kaw* has sounded as you dream, if his wing has touched your shoulder as you walk, he brings you messages from the realm of the spirit and magic is in the air. Note carefully the portents that surround him and see your future revealed as once did the wise of the ancients, but know also that the inexplicable and awesome gather around you.

Listen also to the voices of your mind. They may be messages for a friend or from one, or even from beings far away. Remembering that telepathy is as real as the spoken, like Raven summoning Wolf, act upon what is revealed.

You too have the power to send energies through time and space – strength to an injured companion, love to your partner or one you wish to be connected with. They will unknowingly be receptive to the invisible, and hark to your call.

Dark as the deepest night, Raven's plumage still shines with flashing purple-green iridescence just as the stars sparkle in the sky and coal may be transformed to diamond. For in darkness there is light and all that exists mingles, bringing forth different forms and new shape to the amorphous. As your guide Raven knows you must now discover the enchanter within, for the chance for transformation is yours. Work with the magic of your mind, weave it well, and, renewed, be born into the light.

COUNTERING MALICIOUS TALK · NAVIGATING LIFE

Ray flies through the limitless ocean, her massive flattened sides slowly, rythmically beating like the wings of a mighty underwater bird. Graceful, puissant, wondrous in form and construct, she is one of the blue planet's supreme predators. Ray, like earthly flesh-eaters, has true jaws with teeth. Unlike them, teeth also protrude from her strong flexible body and in Eagle Ray, they have become transformed into defensive spines which can penetrate deep into an aggressor's body, delivering a potent poison.

Teeth help form our words and we too can poison the lives of others through spite, malice, and lies. If you have been attacked by this fearsome weapon and Ray has come to your journeyings, it is to help give you the strength of mind to take heart and cast away the venom that has morphed into destructive thought. If you dwell on it, it will gain strength; if not, its power over your life will diminish daily.

Ray has truly extraordinary senses and powers. The muscles covering two electrical organs within her body form electric plates with a negative underside and positive topside that deliver an electrical shock of more than two hundred volts or two thousand watts. But although Ray delivers death to her prey by this means, her electro-sensory system is far more subtle than this. Ray can detect the presence of creatures buried deep in the sandy floor of her ocean domain by their low-frequency bioelectric fields, but she can also navigate the world. Ray senses not only the kinetic electric fields formed when water moves through the earth's magnetic field, but the gradients of electromotive forces formed by her own powerful gliding path.

Ray can never be lost in the vastness of the blue plane, because her way is always clear. Remnants of this sense still exist within our bodies, and if we listen carefully enough we, too, can navigate through space; but now, Ray has come to help you navigate through time. She counsels that you lose yourself in the rhythmic sound of waves pounding and, as you become as one with the sea, you too will know your way forward.

RHINOCEROS

SAGACITY · SOLITARY CONTEMPLATION

ANCIENT BEHEMOTH, remarkable Rhino first bestrode the lush grasslands and forests which are her home thirty-seven million years ago. Marvellous in design, two-ton Rhino's heavy skin is divided into great protective shields by the massive folds that allow her ease of movement. So tough is this armor that even Tiger and Lion find their razor-sharp claws can gain little purchase, yet Rhino is prey to tiny irritating ticks, and allows her constant companion, Oxpecker bird, to devour them so both may benefit. Standing firm on her pillar-like legs Rhino seems majestic, immovable, but when stirred by anger or intimations of danger by the chirrups of Oxpecker, Rhino, tail curled over her powerful back and head held high, can storm through her lands at up to thirty miles per hour (50 km/h).

Solitary by nature, Rhino spends her days consuming the succulent plants she needs to maintain her great bulk, relaxing in thick, dark, cool mud wallows, and sleeping. Intolerant of disturbance to the calm rhythm of her days, Rhino charges man and beast should they dare to intrude, welcoming only Oxpecker. Repository of ancient wisdoms, Rhino is content, at one with herself. She has no need for society. Sagacious, she stands firm, protected, and secure. Rhino simply is.

She counsels that a life which has no room for contemplation lacks vision and purpose. Formless, life rushes by, dreams scattered and wasted. If Rhino has chosen to guide you it is time to find space in your life to be alone, to still the constant chatter of voices in your head, to take time out from hectic socializing and simply be. At first your mind will echo with a thousand thoughts, a part of you demanding voraciously that you do something, no matter what. Persevere. Consider studying meditation under a skilled master – even Rhino accepts the help of Oxpecker. Your mind will quiet and, as it does so, the true nature of your dreams will make themselves known. They may be very different from the goals you are currently pursuing but they are your truth and now, Rhino advises, you must make them your reality.

SALAMANDER/NEWT

ADMITTING ATTRACTION · THE POWER OF AROMA

Sagacious Salamander, believed by the Renaissance physician Paracesus to be an element-being dwelling in fire, and by the ancients a Fire-Lizard, is a spirit of earth and water, but still truly is a creature of extraordinary powers.

Salamander breathes through her skin, oxygen enters and carbon dioxide is excreted, which confines her to damp environments in trees in the moisture-laden jungles of South America, in damp leaf litter, or even fast flowing streams. Her skin also exudes noxious chemicals – one carries enough neuro-toxin to kill twenty-five thousand of Mouse's kind – its often exotic coloring acting as a warning. Male Salamander excretes potent pheromones to charm his consort.

If Salamander has walked into your world on primordial amphibian limbs, you, too, should be aware of your skin, what it absorbs and what it gives out. You will benefit greatly from aromatherapy massage using natural oils, but Salamander warns against using artificial chemical-based cosmetics whose content may be deleterious to your entire being. We, too, give off inviting sexual pheromones when we desire another, whether we admit it to our conscious selves or not. Observing how others react sexually to you will give you great insight into those your subconscious or inner spirit has chosen, and they may be very different from the bank official or doctor your logical mind has picked. Logic and love do not usually inhabit the same world. Salamander counsels that you consider deeply what you really want from the relationships in your life.

Salamander always returns to the same place to breed, even if she has moved many miles away. She finds her way not through vision or smell, but by using the mystical third eye – her pineal body which detects polarized light – and the orientation of the sun, which she uses as a celestial compass. We, too, possess a pineal gland, which mystical traditions know to be the link between the physical and the spiritual. Crucially, those who would use it can see beyond the material to a higher vision. Like Salamander, see in a different way, using meditation, and find your true spiritual path.

SCARAB BEETLE
WHAT IS UNREGARDED HOLDS A SECRET

Living, armored, shining jewel, Egypt's sacred symbol, Scarab, is the first creature to rise from the earth after the life-giving Nile flood retreats from the delta, its metamorphosis from mummy-like pupae to rude being a magical symbol of death's defeat.

Scarab creates from the waste of others. Like the rays emanating from the rising sun, the points of Scarab's semicircular head dig and cut the dung which is her raw material. Discarding fiber, she creates a sphere from the essential and nutritious elements of the dung, which together with her mate she rolls across the earth to a chamber constructed beneath its surface. Scarab mates, implants the precious fertilized egg in the ball, and covers the chamber with earth. Her child-larva transform first to pupae and finally beetles, who fight through the earth to repeat the cycle of life.

Scarab counsels that you waste nothing and look everywhere. That which others despise may hold within it great riches which are yours to discover. The humble garbage picker takes fresh blooms from wilting garlands which are rewoven to give beauty to another. The sculptor in metal takes the detritus of industry and transforms it into the image of man, of beast, of bird. Scarab asks you to look at everything you normally discard or even despise, for within its form may be hidden the seeds of creation. For some this creation may be procreation. Love, passion, and family may be rejected in favor of the material rewards of career, and Scarab advises that it is time to look within to see if this is truly your path. For others it may be artistic creation as symbolized by the plant seeds in Scarab's ball, which will also blossom.

She also counsels that you look carefully at the people who run through the river of your life. Those unregarded may be the very ones who hold the key to your fulfillment. One may be the catalyst for a new endeavor, whereas another may hold unguessed-at knowledge, or even prove to hold the secret that will unlock your heart.

SCORPION

PASSION · THE CHALLENGE OF PROFOUND EMOTION

ANCIENT, MYSTERIOUS, and imbued with powers of such wonder that she was called on to protect the mighty ancient Egyptian goddess Isis from her enemies, Scorpion inspires reverence and respect in all who know her. Primeval, she represents the creation of life in potent sex as well as its destruction by poison. So puissant are these powers that her cultic images lack her curved venomous tail to protect those who invoke her.

Scorpion does not choose to waste her powers. Her sting is a weapon of self-defense, not offense. She uses sound to warn would-be predators of her power, only killing them as a last resort. Her wisdom is to talk reasonably before striking out and, if needs be, to threaten before taking action – but never to make a threat that she is not prepared to carry out.

Scorpion's courtship dance is tempestuous, complex, and intimate. First, male Scorpion must dance for his consort to establish his role as suitor, not prey to be taken in her voracious pincers. Soon Scorpion responds, and their mutual dance begins. Pincers entwined, they move over the living earth. Scorpion stings his mate passionately, his venom acting not as a toxin but as an aphrodisiac of overwhelming strength. The dance continues. Male Scorpion deposits his spermatophore on the earth. A wild spell of mutual stinging follows, culminating in Scorpion taking his fertility-offering into her ovary. Passion spent, Scorpion lays her eggs. Soon her babies climb her pincers to her back, where their florescence to adulthood begins.

If Scorpion has danced into your journeying, primordial emotions concerned with the very essence of your being are due to be awakened or acknowledged. That her sting can bring both death and passion reminds you that sex, too, can have very different effects on our psyche. At our most vulnerable we can be easily and painfully hurt; at our most passionate, we can be transported into ecstacy. Scorpion reminds you of the deep power of sexual attraction and its properties of transformation and rebirth. Any relationship undertaken with Scorpion by your side will have a profound effect upon your being. She counsels you to accept the challenge.

SEAHORSE

BALANCING MALE AND FEMALE ENERGIES

GRACEFUL, DELICATE, AND TINY – sometimes only a quarter of an inch (6 mm) tall – a coronet adorns Seahorse's elegant head, signal mark of his ancient fishy lineage and the position he once held, drawing mighty Neptune's chariot. Master of camouflage, he lurks unseen in forests of sea grass or great clouds of algae, waiting patiently for the tiny crustaceans that are his prey.

Male Seahorse will fight for his love, his tail wrestling all comers into submission, and is monogamous thereafter. His partner also ignores the seductive blandishments of rivals, discharging her eggs if involved with another. Three days of affectionate courtship are Seahorse's norm. Body colors change at first and heads are rubbed in acknowledgment. They then entwine curved prehensile tails and, anchoring themselves to a blade of grass, where they dance in elaborate ritual. Finally Seahorse shows his mate his empty womb-like brood pouch, for in this culture it is Male Seahorse who falls pregnant. His consort deposits her eggs in his pouch where fertilized, and then embedded in its wall they wax and flourish wondrously. Seahorse changes the fluid within until finally its salinity matches that of the nurturing ocean. His babies, then fully formed, burst into the water on the night of a full silver moon, perfectly adapted to their new home.

If Seahorse has appeared in your dreams swaying to the rhythms of the tides, he is asking you to pay attention to the balance of female and male energies within your being. Male Seahorse, despite nurturing his young and giving birth, is also an ambush predator of the first degree and an aggressive opponent. Seahorse courts his beloved with great energy and persistence.

Seahorse counsels that it is time to develop your female energies to the full, to dive into the depths of profound emotion, to listen quietly to the calling of your psyche and your intuitions, and to allow the side of you that nourishes and nurtures to surface. Walk in the light of the full moon and, like male Seahorse, give birth to all the creativity, fecundity, and feeling that rests within your soul.

MESSAGES IN DREAMS · WORK AND CREATIVITY

Warm-blooded Seal leads a double life. She feeds in the cold, watery depths, but woos, has sex, and gives birth on rocky terrain or on thick shelves of ice. So at home in water is this close relative of earthly carnivores such as Bear that asleep, she rises from the comfort of the ocean floor to breathe and then, still dreaming, glides gently back to her sandy bed.

Seal has made many adaptations to live as she does. Her limbs have transformed to flippers, her tail shortened, her neck elongated, and her spine made supple. Agile and undulating in water, she is now ungainly on land – her fur exchanged for heat-insulating blubber that is three inches (7.5 cm) thick, her eyes rounded like fish, those natural denizens of the deep.

Water, from which life on land sprang, speaks of imagination, intuition, the power of dreams, and the infinity of creation. That Seal bears her pups on earth shows these landscapes of the mind may be made material, but not without some sacrifice. If Seal is now guiding you, your dreams may be vivid, long, and important to your life. On awakening, scribe their content and study their symbolism in your world. Do they show desires not yet acknowledged? Seal counsels that it is time to make your dreams your own, whatever they may be.

Seal suckles her fleshly creations on warm milk, rich with fifty percent fat, so that they may grow robustly, exuberantly, and survive in a harsh environment. She advises that the fertile knowledge that feeds your inspiration must itself be nourished by wide research, and that although this may then become a period of unparalleled inspiration for you, no true creation comes without hard work and dedication.

For an idea to have form, the technical ability for its execution must also be honed. The artist may need to spend many years perfecting her craft before something of true beauty can emerge, and often forgo the society of friends and family in its service. The wisdom of Seal may be challenging, but its rewards are great. Ultimately, however, only you can decide whether or not to follow your magical teacher.

SKUNK

SELF–RESPECT BRINGS OTHERS' RESPECT

Two vivid white stripes run from Skunk's white blazoned head to meet again on her long, impressively furred tail. Skunk, peaceable in her spirit, amiable in her wanderings, is gently warning potential adversaries to stay out of her way and treat her with respect. Even when predators approach, Skunk does not immediately employ her noxious, debilitating perfume, but employs an impressive armory of other behavioral threats. She arches her back, hair bristling, and walks to her foe showing no fear; she stamps her feet, hisses savagely, clicks her teeth, and finally performs a handstand with tail raised as a clear message of intent. If her adversary still persists, Skunk delivers a blast of oily sulphur alcohol, a potent musk, intensely nauseating and excruciatingly irritating, which creatures great and small remember graphically. Few care to repeat the encounter.

Skunk is secure, her reputation precedes her, so she rarely has need to defend herself. If she has strolled self-assuredly into your dreams or journeying, it is to ask you how you deal with other people. She counsels that those with self-respect have no need to fly off the handle, as their very presence demands regard from others. If the people around you are not treating you as you would wish, and you feel constantly angry with them, Skunk advises that it is time to look inside as your self-esteem must sadly be low. Skunk knows that we are all valuable – take the time to consider all the great things about yourself and turn to the world with a new face. It will treat you well.

Skunk can attract and repel as musk has potent sexual connotations – perfumes and pheromones can be heady aphrodisiacs. Skunk counsels that you possess the sexual power to send clear, attractive messages to others. However, as Skunk targets her musk, you, too, should be careful where you send this energy or risk enchanting those whom you find undesirable as well as those whom you feel passion for. And don't let your own energies blind you to those who send their sexual energy to you, for within their ranks may be the one who also holds the power of love.

SLOTH

LIVING IN HARMONY · RECOGNIZING THE PRECIOUS

HUMANKIND GAVE SLOTH this name, seeing in the apparent stillness of her neo-tropical rainforest life something considered a Deadly Sin – laziness and a profound dislike of work. But Sloth is virtue incarnate, a living, breathing, perfect eco-system – the ultimate embodiment of sustainability, of recycling, of living in harmony with Gaia, the earth. And Sloth flourishes, her population denser than that of any other mammal. Instead of ranging noisily and energetically through the forest in search of food like Monkey or Parrot, Sloth prefers to dine on what is near at hand – thick, green leaves. Although abundant, leaves contain little nutrition, and even after the hard-working bacteria in Sloth's stomach have wrought their transforming magic, there are few vitamins and even fewer calories for Sloth to lavish on activity. But Sloth's needs are small.

She defecates once a week, making the long journey to the forest floor to do so, digging a hole to bury her faeces under her favorite tree, both fertilizing it and recycling its nutriments. Hooks growing from her toes allow her to hang upside down without using any muscles at all. At speed she may move at five-and-a-half yards (5 m) an hour, but what use has Sloth of such energy-consuming locomotion? Secure in the canopy, she possesses no predators, unless warming herself in treetop sunshine she is perhaps espied by Eagle. Jaguar is defeated, unable to reach beneath her branch, and leaves, her quarry, do not run away. But still, Sloth's super-long neck twists two-hundred-and-seventy degrees, allowing her to look forward through the forest gloom – just in case – even when upside down.

If gentle Sloth has dreamily materialized in your journeyings, she wishes you to consider the benefits of her ways. Sloth is impregnable, proof to those much stronger and more active than her; she wants for nothing and wastes nothing. Treasure that which surrounds you, remembering that even a plastic bag is manufactured from irreplaceable oil that has taken aeons to form from a once-living tree. Squander neither love nor the material, even if they are no longer new and while like Sloth, keeping watch, relax in true prosperity.

SNAIL

OVERCOMING HARSH CONDITIONS

SNAIL FLOURISHES IN both suburban garden and scalding black water belched from molten rock below the ocean's floor alike. In this underwater vent, at a temperature of 750 degrees Fahrenheit (around 260° C) and a pressure of two hundred and fifty times that on land, extraordinary gastropod Snail uses what is at hand to protect herself from fearsome predators and constructs her scales from iron sulphides, literally creating metal armor-plating. If Snail has come on her clear silvery path, contracting and stretching her one great foot as she moves slowly but determinedly by your side as you journey, it is to assure you that you, too, can protect yourself from the harshest enemies or unworthy critics – like Snail, you merely need to think laterally.

Nautilus Snail also lives in the world's oceans, but in the more forgiving, vividly colored and exotic environment of the coral reefs of the western Pacific. A creature of exquisite loveliness, the proportions of her shell accord to phi or, as it is more usually called, the golden mean. This is a mathematical ratio of 1 to 1.618 used by Leonardo da Vinci and probably by the ancients before him, a formula frequently used in architecture and other disciplines because it is perceived by the human mind as aesthetically pleasing. As this ratio goes to thousands of decimal points, its true and absolute beauty can never be attained, but it can always be strived for. Nautilus Snail, therefore lives within great beauty, for her shell is her home. She counsels that you, too, strive to live in an environment that embodies what you personally find aesthetically pleasing.

Our day-to-day living space effects our state of mind much more than we realize. If our garden plants are scraggy and dying, the colors on our walls dim and fading, our lighting cold and unfriendly, we too feel less than positive and optimistic. Like Nautilus Snail, our homes should be inviting and lovely. A bunch of wild flowers in glass, a lampshade that imparts a soft light, and even a spring-clean can all change how we feel and how others feel about us.

SPIDER

TRAVEL · CREATIVITY · THE POWER OF TOUCH

For four hundred million years Spider has spun her exquisite, multifaceted, magical silk – more elastic than nylon, stronger than its equivalent in steel – in every conceivable environment except the central Antarctic cap.

She flies to remote islands and uninhabited lands on strands of silk let loose into the air reaching heights of sixteen thousand feet (4,900 m) and journeying hundreds, even thousands, of miles through azure skies and dark, brooding storms.

If Spider has chosen to guide you it is time to expand your horizons metaphorically and literally. Travel to faraway lands or a neighboring town, to a wild flower meadow you have never visited before. See the world through new eyes and understand deep within that nothing is impossible. If you have always longed to live in a different world or in a different way, Spider counsels that the time may have come to make this dream reality.

Spider sees her world through touch, not light, translating vibrations in air, earth, and web into knowledge. She advises that you, too, take wisdom from what you cannot see and if the fleeting touch of another affects you, acknowledge that connection and encourage it to flourish.

From the silk on which she sails Spider also weaves her geometric spiral web, symbol of all creativity. Spider's silk comes from deep within her body, a liquid substance that hardens and takes form as she stretches and pulls it into her desired form. So the seeds of creation lie within your essence, but like Spider you must toil to bring them to light to turn imaginings into beauty. Spider's body is itself the figure-of-eight shape that symbolizes infinity and implicit within this, limitless creation. With Spider to guide you, your efforts will not be in vain. Hidden in Spider's web, in its angles and lines, its geometric form, is the basis of a primordial alphabet that in mythology Spider wrought for man. As the written word transformed humankind it may transform you, and the knowledge or insights that you disseminate through this medium have the potential to bring both change and enlightenment to others.

SQUIRREL

INVESTMENT IN THE FUTURE · CHANGE

Squirrel scurries through woods and towns from Scotland to India, her lively presence missing only in Australasia. Unlike other mammal guides, benevolent Squirrel makes herself familiar to humankind so that all may share in her special wisdom, that of preparing for the future. If she has chosen now to also appear in your dreams or journeying, or given you a special sign, it is imperative you heed her call – for change really is in the air.

Combining the skills of the trapeze and high-wire artist as she traverses the trees and creepers of her aerial home, Squirrel is athletic and bursting with energy, and counsels that you, too, hone your physical being. Change consumes energy and the more of it you have stored, the more easily you may deal with what is to come.

Always humming, always busy, Squirrel never wastes her time as she prepares for winter and the lean times it brings. Nuts store well in the cool earth of winter and squirrel can scent them a foot under snow and deep in the ground – a larder worth defending territory for – and she may defend its rich fruiting tree. But when the pollen-laden cones of the Douglas Fir lie heavily and temptingly on its branches, Squirrel, knowing that there is abundance for all and that these cones do not store well, shares the tree's bounty and dines well.

She advises that you gather skills that are universal, transferable, fundamental – the simple tools of life, such as cooking or the growing of vegetables, too often cast aside in a metropolitan world – and that you also preserve some of today's material bounty for ever-changing times. Squirrel caches only what she needs, and knows that the weight of excess material goods and their constant acquisition anchors us firmly in our past and depletes our energy. We need to be light and adaptable both to swim with tides of the future and, like Squirrel, enjoy what is here today.

SWAN

THE CONTAINING OF OPPOSITES

Swan, most beautiful of waterfowl, snowy-white, symbolic embodiment of purity, is a creature of dichotomy. Until the rest of Gaia discovered Australia, Black Swan was a mythical being, a creature of unattainable rarity and in folk traditions cloaked in evil. But Black Swan, scarlet-beaked and exquisite in plumage of sparkling jet, proved the impossible to be possible and was considered so fabulous that she was known as the ancestor of the Bibbulmen, an aborigine tribe. Elegant and graceful of form, Swan can yet break the arm of man with her mighty wing or drown Fox beneath it should either transgress her domain.

If Swan has flown mightily into your journeyings, she comes to tell you that sweet loveliness can hold within it strength and fierce offense without losing its own wondrous quality – and to let no other convince you otherwise. And to know, as she does, that you can attain the impossible dream because it already exists. Swim with the river of your life, and it will be revealed.

Swan is faithful and demonstrative of her love. During first courtship they greet one other with breasts touching and heads turned and, when they have decided to bond for life, honor their decision with a triumph display of "raised wings and fluffed neck feathers"* and calling. Sexual invitation is accompanied by much preening and head-dipping, and its conclusion celebrated with muted trumpet while the partners, breast to breast, half-rise from their watery bridal-bed, necks stretched to the skies. Swan and her consort then relax together and indulge in a little bathing, preening, and tail-wagging.

Swan reveals the importance of sexuality in a long-term bond and counsels that it is a manifestation of true devotion – its form irrelevant. In legend, Swan attains the form of a virginal maid, when she slips from her dress of feathers and is often taken by man for his wife. Male gods, such as Zeus, take her long-necked phallic form to ravish. Innocence and experience, female and male, seducer and seduced, Swan contains all these contrasts as do we. What is important is that we express them in love. And that is the wisdom of Swan.

* The Swans, Peter Scott and the Wildlife Trust,

TIGER

HOT PASSION • TRUST THROUGH FAIRNESS

Supreme ruler of the eastern jungles, Tiger is svelte power incarnate. No creature is more charismatic, no beast more beautiful, than sleek Tiger, silently moving through lush jungle foliage. Muscles ripple beneath taut skin and peerless coat, dark diagonals slash through golden russet fur, greeny-yellow eyes blaze. So vivid, so eye-catching to us, but in her natural environment these complex and intricate markings are perfect camouflage and allow her to silently ambush her prey.

Magical in her ability to remain invisible until she strikes her prey, as your guide Tiger counsels that you too hide your precious plans until you are ready to implement them, lest others choose to thwart you or steal your ideas. She also advises that you take no more than your due from others. Tiger kills only what she needs, and every denizen of the forest knows this. If she has eaten, even timid Deer will drink with her, confident of her safety. Friends and prospective business or creative partners alike will flock to you, too, if they know that they can trust you.

Like all sovereign predators, Tiger is always accompanied by her Crow-species familiar, Magpie, Crow, and Raven. Her kills provide them with food and they are her constant companions in play, so much may be gained from studying the wisdom of these ancient feathered messengers. Alone among the big cats, Tiger inhabits the earth and the water, partaking of all the latter element's primeval mystical power. Moving effortlessly between worlds, she reminds you of the Shaman's ability to journey and consider problems through different eyes and from different angles.

No creature is more sensuous than Tiger. She luxuriates in jungle pools, stretches languidly in the humidity of the tropics, and announces her fertility by scent-marking the borders of her territory with a pungent fluid and roaring lustily until one or more males are summoned. Tiger's sudden presence in your reality can betoken the arrival of passion or desire, the bright rekindling of a relationship in which you have been taken for granted, or the arrival of one or more ardent lovers.

TORTOISE

ANCIENT WISDOM · REMAINING TRUE TO ONESELF

Tortoise evolved two hundred and twenty million years ago, her beautiful shell artistically fashioned from her strong ribs and dermal bone uniquely protecting the soft vulnerable flesh within. When the planet was young, before flowers blossomed, mammals suckled their young, birds flew through cavernous skies, or snakes slithered, Tortoise walked majestically on rock, sand, and earth. Dinosaur burgeoned, ruled, and perished. Tortoise marched unhurriedly on through time and still plods slowly through space – a perfect living masterpiece – the embodiment of ancient wisdom.

From the beginnings of recorded history the Chinese recognized the innate power and sagaciousness of Tortoise, appointing her guardian of the heaven's northern quadrant and using her shell to presage the future. If Tortoise has stepped into your dreams on determined hoary feet, look to the timeless wisdom of ages, which she will guide you toward. Within its lore are the answers to problems that beset you today. Tortoise also counsels that change for the sake of novelty is now to be resisted, and advises that you remain true to your way of living, your partner, your creative dream, lest you destroy something which is more wonderful than you yet know.

Tortoise's ultraslow metabolism conserves life energy – she lives for two hundred years, sometimes more. The great height of her carapace ensures her invulnerability from the ravening jaws of predators, while the ability to withdraw her head within her shell makes her physical being virtually impregnable. Living in a fast, ruthless world in which the demands of fashion cause people to reshape their bodies through surgery and status symbols are used to assess their worth, rather than the quality of their characters and souls, is wearing and hard. These superficial values are ephemeral but the veiled barbs and open criticisms of those who wish you to subscribe to them can still wound. Like Tortoise, construct a mental carapace to protect yourself and remain true to your own being. Never forget that just as Tortoise's hatchlings emerge from their shells, perfect, you too were born flawless.

VULTURE/CONDOR

PURIFICATION · LIVING WITHOUT CAUSING HARM

SUBLIME VULTURE WAITS for the warmth of the life-giving sun before beating her great wings and taking to the skies, searching for the thermals upon which, in great circles, she can rise. When she reaches its summit she dives across the skies, sometimes reaching sixty miles per hour (96 km/h), until she reaches another pocket of rising warm air. Hour after hour Vulture glides the skies without even flapping her wings, taking her energy from the sun itself, until she sees her nourishment on the earth below. If Vulture has silently streamed into the skyscape of your dreams, consider the cares in your life. Are you weighed down by the cares of the mundane or, like Vulture, does your spirit soar? She tells you that it is now time to set yourself free.

Unlike other creatures, Vulture harms nothing. Fruit trees need not fear her passing, nor Rabbit. Corn ripens richly on its stalk, and Goat need have no fear for her kid, for Vulture eats only the flesh of that which has died or has been killed by another. Vulture thrives on that which is given to her. Her spirit is benign indeed.

Vulture purifies the world of flesh that might putrefy and become a source of disease – the acid in her stomach is so strong that it dissolves bone and kills botulism and cholera, scourges that devastate humankind. She shows the oneness of life and death, the interconnectedness of all, and the constancy of change. Mut, ancient Egyptian Vulture goddess, mother from which all of creation springs, takes the form of Vulture who from the dead brings forth life and who in her flesh-and-blood form is the most devoted of mothers. A solid may turn immediately to gas in chemistry; in alchemy, this transformation from the fixed to the volatile is symbolized by Vulture.

Protective in her maternal nature, Vulture has come to reassure you that transformation is inevitable, that from the depths of despair may spring forth joy. Be like Vulture, accept what is given, and see life renewed and fresh.

WALRUS

ARDOR AND INDIFFERENCE COMPETE

Bulky behemoth of the pristine Arctic, Walrus weighs up to two-and-a-half thousand pounds (1150 kg) while massive offensive canines, three feet (0.9 m) long, extend downward from his mighty jaw. These he uses like ice picks to propel himself over the ocean's craggy bed and polar ice alike, aided by his flippers which he turns backwards. As Walrus gets older he becomes even weightier, his tusks more solid. It is a rare pretender to his throne that will risk his wrath, for to have survived long he is a skilled fighter indeed. No other spirits threaten Walrus. So potent is he that even Orca – killer whale – fears his coming. In homage to his power, Inuit, threatened by Orca while on the seas, imitate his enraged bellowing call into the deep waters. Orca, dismayed, swims away.

A harem master beyond compare, Walrus may have as many as one hundred females in his territory, and he has exclusive mating rights. Walrus's genes stretch far into the evolutionary future, ensuring his earthly immortality.

A creature of pre-eminent passion and absolute power, if Walrus has swum mightily into your world you must question the position of these two fundamental tenets in your life. Are you overbearing with those to whom you are newly attracted, or your long-term partner? Do you deny the importance of yearning and ardor in your life? Do you let others' passions dominate you? When Walrus basks in the midnight sun of his Arctic domain he appears bright reddish brown – a lusty symbol of his inner self. This is because to keep cool he must dilate his blood vessels, allowing cool air to carry away excess heat from his body so fabulously insulated with glorious blubber. When he dives in the freezing ocean he withdraws blood from his surface, keeping his body above the water at a temperature of one hundred degrees Fahrenheit (35° C). He now appears pale and white, and symbolically his ardor has cooled.

Walrus offsets these extremes of temperature, and so must you. In a relationship of passion, the balance of power is everything. Walrus counsels that it is time for you to seek equilibrium.

WATER BUFFALO

RECLAIMING INNER STRENGTH · WALKING LIGHTLY

W ATER BUFFALO SWIMS in India's sacred waters to cool her massive, comfortable, slatey-black body, and wallows languidly in refreshing mud. Her milk, thick and rich, makes creamy white golden butter and melting cheese. But Buffalo's placid maternal exterior belies her wild and tempestuous nature. She charges when approached if the mood is upon her, and shows no hesitation in attacking and frequently besting even wild India's supreme ruler, Tiger. She saunters boldly into man's fields to avail herself of luscious juicy crops, and defiantly ignores his protests. Buffalo's nature is never tamed, nor her courage dimmed, for even her domestic self faces Tiger undaunted and stubbornly wanders where she will. Buffalo faces life head-on and tosses her enemies determinedly behind her.

Unlike Monkey's deft prehensile hands and feet, or the sheathed weapons that are Panther's paws, Buffalo's feet are exquisitely designed for walking. Cloven-hoofed, she walks on the tips of two toes, each one embedded in protective horn, while the corresponding foot bones are fused together for stability. Buffalo weighs two thousand pounds (900 kg), but walks nimbly on unforgiving rock and effortlessly through boggy marsh. Like Buffalo, walk lightly through life and you, too, may go where you will.

If Buffalo has come into your dreams, it is time to consider the measure of your own spirit and courage. When Lion seeks to predate African Buffalo's calves she drives Lion into the hopeful shelter of whispering-leaved trees and keeps her there, helpless as a stranded kitten. Lion, if she survives, learns a salutary lesson, and Buffalo garners respect.

Tragedy, disappointment, hardship, failure, even abuse, are intrinsic to living and can knock the very breath from our bodies. Sometimes, however, we remain cowed by events, unable to move forward, frightened of what lies ahead; of what others, or life, may inflict upon us. Mighty crescent-horned Buffalo is the brave spirit within your soul waiting to be reclaimed. It is time to take your courage in both hands and dare to be.

WEASEL

THE POWER OF SILENCE · ACTING INDEPENDENTLY

Long, slinky carnivore, bright-eyed Weasel is mistress of secrecy and silence and the fine art of dissembling. Her slender body slips easily into the welcoming tiny cracks and crevices that act as doorways to her dens, making her safe from fatter more glossy predators who would dine on her toothsome body. However, she may with ease pursue Pica into her tiny rocky retreat, and tracks Mouse relentlessly through her tunnels, and so Weasel rarely knows the pangs of hunger.

If she has zigzagged into your life, you too can squash into inaccessible places – the oversubscribed study course, the last seat on a flight to Japan. Weasel counsels that you forget the self-defeating attitude which groans "What's the point? So many people will apply..." and, like Weasel, tirelessly pursue your prey.

Weasel is rarely what she seems. She confuses even Hawk, sharp-eyed master of the skies who strikes at her tail's black tip believing it to be her head, so leaving Weasel free to prowl through another deceitful day. She snakes with lightning speed into rocky fissure and woody cleft. Was she ever there at all? Ermine Weasel turns white as the crispest snow when winter powders her territory, invisible to all. And silence, one of her most potent weapons, masks ferocity, cunning intelligence, and keen observation.

As your guide Weasel counsels that you, too, should not always be what you seem, and asks you to consider the great strength inherent in subtlety and silence. It traps others into underestimating your powers and induces them to reveal far more than they might otherwise, through talking garrulously and behaving injudiciously. Having revealed their hand, the advantage is all yours. In business and love alike, observe the game and, like scent-conscious Weasel, ask yourself if things smell right or if there is intrigue floating in the air.

Weasel is solitary; no team player, she advises that partnerships and coalitions in board room and bedroom alike will dissolve your power and dilute your creative force. Throw aside self-doubt and reliance on others and be like Weasel, one of the most successful creatures of earth.

WHALE

TRANSFORMATION THROUGH SOUND

THROUGH TROPICAL OCEAN and Arctic sea, Whale, denizen of the deep, swims slowly, steadily, majestically, as becomes one of such ancient lineage. Traveling twelve thousand five hundred miles in a solar year, she plots her course from landmarks on the water's floor and the land's coast and by the sun, the moon, and the stars. Was she really brought to earth from the mystical constellation of Sirius? Is it there she looks for guidance as she voyages through the blue? Only whale knows for sure.

In water light travels thickly for short distances and perfumes and scents are diluted and dissolved, so Whale communicates by song and the myriad sounds that are a language humankind cannot as yet understand. These travel over a hundred miles (160 km) and at five times their speed in the air. Humpback Whale sings for thirty minutes – a love serenade of his own – a composition of great complexity with recurring themes. He tells his love of his experience, prowess, and wisdom so that she may recognize him from afar. Over time his song undergoes great changes, a reflection of his ever-evolving spirit. Those whom Whale has chosen to guide should pay great attention to all the sounds and echoes of their world and those of other planes, developing the clairaudient ability that Whale knows lies deep within.

Music has always wrought great change in living creatures. Whale's wisdom is that rhythm, vibration, and frequency may heal both body and soul. The chanting of Buddhists, the beat of the Shamanic drum as you journey, can bring to you the celestial harmony of the eternal spheres and have the power to change your consciousness and your physical being forever. Whale knows that in modern times humans rarely use their voices, except to talk. The cry of triumph, the song of joy, the scream that releases tension, all die before they find utterance, inhibited by the fear that others may think us mad or sad. Whale's wisdom is to take back your voice and grow stronger and lighter as its magic transforms your mind.

WOLF

RELEASING THE SPIRIT · SELF-KNOWLEDGE

W OLF HAS BEEN our ancient companion in the struggle to survive, a symbol of all that is wild and free. Like all top predators, Wolf keeps the environment healthy and in balance. When he chases Caribou herds through the northern wilderness, his paws crunching on crisp virgin snow, his calm intelligence works in tandem with other members of the pack to single out a weak member of the herd for the kill. Wolf must pounce on every opportunity or starve. Respecting the sacrifice Caribou has made, Wolf wastes nothing. He eats until the bones are as white and clean as the frosted icicles that hang on the heavy pines and then returns home to share his bounty with the pack's hungry growing pups or adult wolves who were unable to hunt through infirmity or old age.

Wolf is a powerful, untamed spirit because he remains true to his nature. He knows himself and understands the true extent of his extraordinary physical, mental, and psychic powers, but also understands his weaknesses. His life depends on this. In an urban setting, our lives also can hang in the balance, sometimes literally in the flash of a knife drawn by an assailant, sometimes metaphorically as we struggle to survive in an environment that is harsh in different ways from that inhabited by Wolf. As your guide, he comes with love to teach you much: that you will only flourish if you are yourself, untamed and unbowed; that awareness of your powers means that you can respect your intuition on a dark, lonely street, and survive; to trust in those you instinctively recognize as meaningful in your life. Like Wolf, share what you have in compassion and mutual benefit that creativity may be forged from failure, that opportunities should never be wasted, and that nature, of which man is a part, must be in balance. Wolf takes what he needs, no more, no less. He counsels that you do the same for his future, and for yours.

WOODPECKER

ETHICAL LIVING · RELATING TO OTHERS

Heartbeat of the earth, Woodpecker has drummed out her message in the world's woodlands for over fifty million years. The Ktunaxa, a native North American tribe believe that Woodpecker Yamakpah was sent to the earth to safeguard humanity, and a crucial element of this is her ancient role as guardian of the forests. Trees are the lungs of our land – their roots prevent mudslides and flooding, and they provide us with everything from wine corks to bookcases, lacquer to paper. From Brazil to Norway trees support the web of life to which we too belong. Unremitting deforestation causes constant extinctions and is altering Gaia in ways that ultimately may be irreversible. Species of Woodpecker herself are already gone forever.

If Woodpecker has tapped loudly as you dream, it is time to consider the sustainability of your lifestyle. Do you consume without thought? Do you buy furniture hacked from trees clear cut from the world's last ancient woodlands? Once they supported beauty and complexity, bird, insect, and beast. Now sterile, incased in concrete, they can create and sustain no more. Do you bin paper and plastic, consume petrol extravagantly, wasting the irreplaceable fruitfulness of trees past and present? Woodpecker counsels that by safeguarding the forests and being aware of how you live, you safeguard yourself and your children's future. Consumerism can never bring the peace and fulfillment that fundamentally we all crave – it is a passion founded on emptiness. The fiery red always found on the head of Woodpecker is a reminder of real passions, those for our lovers, our friends, the causes close to our heart, a dear animal, a meadow in bloom. As your guide, she counsels that these are the fires to follow in life, the rhythms to sway to.

Woodpecker's drumming also has deeply mystical implications. Akin to that of the Shamans, steady and relentless in its beat, for those whom Woodpecker has chosen to guide it signals that journeying may prove to be an extraordinarily enlightening experience, even life-changing. Some may discover within themselves a wonderful and unguessed-at power that can be harnessed for the Shamanic healing of others.

NOTES TO INTRODUCTION

1 *Shamanism*, Mircea Eliade, Princetown University Press, 1970.

2 *The Shaman*, Piers Vitebsky, Duncan Baird, London 2001.

3 *Shamanism*, Mircea Eliade, Princetown University Press, 1970, page 67.

4 *The Way of the Shaman*, Michael Harner, HarperCollins New York, 1990.

5 *Shamanism*, Mircea Eliade, Princetown University Press, 1970; quoting Parteneon, p. 150

6 *The Way of the Shaman*, Michael Harner, HarperCollins New York, 1990, p. 66.

7 *The Way of the Shaman*, Michael Harner, HarperCollins New York, 1990.

8 *Shamanism*, Mircea Eliade, Princetown University Press, 1970; quoting Castagné, p. 97.

9 *Vocalizing in the house cat, a phonetic and functional study*, M. Moelk, *American Journal of Psychology*, vol. 57 1944, p. 18.

BIBLIOGRAPHY

The Apes V. Reynolds, Cassell 1968

The New Encyclopaedia of Insects and their Allies O'Toole 2002

The Badgers of the World C. A. Long and C. A. Killingley, C. C. Thomas 1983

The Last Panda G. Schaller, University of Chicago Press 1998

The New Encylopaedia of Reptiles and Amphibians, Halliday and Alder, OUP 2002

The Prezevalasky Horse Dr S. Bokonyi, Souvenir 1974

Horses and Grasses P. Duncan, Springer-Verlag 1992

Track of the Coyote T. Wilkinson, North Word Press 1995

Shamanism M. Eliade, Princeton University Press 1970

Animal Social Complexity F. B. M de Wall, P. L. Tyak (eds), Harvard University Press 2003

The Crows Coombs, Batsford 1978

Kingdom of the Octopus F. W. Lane, Jarrolds 1957

A Neotropical Companion J. Kricher, Princeton University Press 1989

The Swans P. Scott and the Wildlife Trust, Michael Joseph 1972

Wild Wonders of Rajasthan V. D. Sharma Rajpal Singh, Prakash Books 2000

The Book of Indian Animals S. H. Prater, OUP India 1998

Mammals of North America Adrian Forsyth, Firefly Buffalo 1999

The Life of Birds D. Attenborough, BBC 1998

The Salmon J. W Jones, Collins 1959

Sociobiology E. O. Wilson, Harvard 1979

The Life of the Kookaburra W. Eastmen, Angus and Robertson 1970

Wild Geese of the World M. Owen, Batsford 1980

Land of the Tiger Valmik Thapar, BBC 1997

Behavior Guide to African Mammals, R. Despard Estes, University of California 1991

The Way of the Shaman Michael Harner, HarperCollins San Francisco 1990

The Teachings of Don Juan Carlos Castenada, University of California Press 1968

A Separate Reality Carlos Castenada, Simon & Schuster 1971

Journey to Iktan Carlos Castenada, Simon & Schuster 1972

What Good are Bugs? G. Waldbauer, Harvard University Press

Medicine Cards Jamie Sams and David Carson, Bear & Co. 1988

The Life of Mammals D. Attenborough, BBC

The Fascination of Reptiles M. Richardson, Andre Deutsch 1972

Animal Speak Ted Andrews, Llewelyn 2003

Of Wolves and Men B. Lopez, Simon & Schuster 1982

Mech, David, and Boitani, Luigi eds. *Wolves, behaviour ecology and conservation,* University of Chicago Press 2003

The Shaman Piers Vitebsky, Duncan Baird Publications 2001

Biophilia Edward O. Wilson, Harvard University Press 2003

Birds in Legend: Fable & Folklore Ernest Ingersoll, Longmans Green & Co 1923

Shamanism: The Spirit World of Korea ed. Chai-shin Yu and R. Guisso Vol1 Asian Humanities Press, 1988

Shamanism as a Spiritual Practice for Daily Life T. Cowan, The Crossing Press 1996

The Magic of Shapeshifting Rosalyn Greene, Weiser Books 2000

Tiger! Kailish Sankhala, Collins 1978

Art of the Amur Okladinikov, Harry H. Abrams, Aurora Art Publishers 1981

RESOURCES

Here are just a handful of organizations that work tirelessly to preserve our environment and the creatures within it. They all recognize that we are a part of the web of life, and are dependent upon it.

If you possibly can, take the time to look at these websites and perhaps help them make the world a place that is happier and healthier for us all.

Environmental Investigation Agency
Exposes illegal trade in timber, skins, and body parts, and strives to preserve the few wild animals left in the world.

EIA USA
PO Box 53343
Washington DC 20009, USA

Tel: 202 483 6621
Fax: 202 986 8626
Email: usinfo@eia-international.org

EIA UK
62/63 Upper Street
London N1 0NY, UK

Tel: 020 7354 7960
Fax: 020 7354 7961
http://www.eia-international.org
Email: ukinfo@eia-international.org

SPANA
Spana (Society for the Protection of Animals Abroad) works to give free vetinary help to animals such as camels and donkeys who help some of the world's poorest people survive. The Society operates in Algeria, Morocco, Tunisia, Jordan, Syria, Mali, Mauritania, and Ethiopia.

14 John Street
London WC1N 2EB, UK

Tel: 44 (0) 207 831 3999
Fax: 44 (0) 207 831 5999
Email: hq@spana.org
www.spana.org

Tiger Trust
The Tiger Trust's mission is to save the tiger and preserve its natural habitat in India.

206 Rakeshdeep, 11 Commercial Complex
Gulmohar Enclave
New Delhi 110049, India

Tel: 91 11 6853760/6858656
Fax: 91 11 6865212
Email: info@adventure-india.com

Save the Tiger Fund
The Save the Tiger Fund (STF), a program of the National Fish and Wildlife Foundation, is dedicated to supporting the conservation of Asia's remaining wild tigers.

1120 Connecticut Ave, NW, Suite 900
Washington, DC 20036, USA

Telephone: (202) 857-0166
Fax: (202) 857-0162 fax
www.5tigers.org

Greenpeace International
Campaigning organization that aims to
ensure the earth's ability to nurture life in
all its diversity.

Ottho Heldringstraat 5
1066 A2 Amsterdam
Netherlands

Tel: 31 20 718 2000
Fax: 31 20 514 8151
Email:
supporter.services@int.greenpeace.org
www.greenpeace.org

www.shamanism.org
Michael Harner's Foundation for
Shamanic Studies. Shamanic journeying
CDs are also available from this website.

National Resources Defense Council
NRDC is an American non-profit
organization with 550,000 members and a
staff of lawyers, scientists, and other
environmental specialists. The
organization's mission is to safeguard the
earth – its people, plants, and animals,
and the natural systems upon which all
life depends.

40 West 20th St
New York, NY 10011, USA

Tel: (212) 7272 2700
www.nrdc.org

INDEX

ACKNOWLEDGMENTS

I would like to thank my publisher, Cindy Richards, for staying on it through thick and thin and for all her generous help; my editor, Liz Dean, for patience, understanding, and wisdom; Nick for manning the Cico fort, and all the rest of the team who work so hard. I would also like to thank Csaba Pázstor for his beautiful illustrations which so perfectly capture the spirit of the wild creatures around us.

This book is dedicated to every person on every continent who strives to preserve the wild places of the earth and the creatures who live within them and who understands that objects do not have souls. And to my dog, Poppy, who in accordance with medieval lore has faithfully sat at my feet, symbolizing wisdom and knowledge, and has been my muse and ambassador to the wilder, wider world.

IMAGE CREDITS